C000084619

Landscapes of
IRELAND

a countryside guide
Fourth edition

Peter Singer

SUNFLOWER BOOKS

Fourth edition
Copyright © 2010
Sunflower Books™
PO Box 36160
London SW7 3WS, UK

ISBN 978 1 85691 385 0

Signpost, Beara Peninsula

Important note to the reader

We have tried to ensure that the descriptions and maps in this book are error-free at press date. The book will be updated, where necessary, whenever future printings permit. It will be very helpful for us to receive your comments (sent in care of the publishers, please) for the updating of future printings.

We also rely on those who use this book — especially walkers — to take along a good supply of common sense when they explore. *Storm damage, erosion or flooding may make a route unsafe at any time*. If the route is not as we outline it here, and your way ahead is not secure, return to the point of departure. *Never attempt to complete a tour or walk under hazardous conditions!* Please read carefully the notes on pages 69 to 77, as well as the introductory comments at the beginning of each tour and walk (regarding road conditions, equipment, grade, distances and time, etc). Explore *safely*, while at the same time respecting the beauty of the countryside.

Cover photograph: Ross Castle, Muckross Lake, Killarney (Car tour 6 and Walk 8)
Title page: pub in Dingle

Sunflower Books and 'Landscapes' are Registered Trademarks.
Photographs: cover: Hermann Knapp; pages 4, 6, 13, 16-17, 27, 40-41, 42 (left), 45 (bottom left), 48 (bottom left and top right), 50-51, 62-63, 64 (top), 80-81, 84-85, 95, 111, 114, 119: Andreas Stieglitz; all other photographs: the author
Maps: adapted from from the 1:50,000 Discovery/Discoverer Series; © Ordnance Survey of Ireland and © Crown Copyright
A CIP catalogue record for this book is available from the British Library.
Printed and bound in China: WKT Company Ltd

10 9 8 7 6 5 4 3 2 1

Contents

4   Landscapes of Ireland

Brandon Point, Dingle Peninsula (Car tour 7)

Preface

Ireland is a country of unmatchable landscapes that never fail to give you a satisfying sense of discovery — from the magnificently wooded Killarney lakeland to the stark moonscapes of the Burren, from the sheer cliffs, exposed headlands and sand-fringed coves of the indented west coast to the wild misty hills in Donegal, from the dazzling Giant's Causeway to secluded loughs hidden in turf-laden mountains.

The moody weather changes Ireland's landscapes from one minute to the next. Walk along a wind-swept promontory on a misty day, with a raging sea pounding the cliffs, and you really *feel* the force of nature. All of a sudden the sun breaks through the clouds, bathing the surroundings in brilliant light. Verdant pastures hang precipitously over the coastal cliffs, with soft grey islets gradually emerging from the mists. On a balmy summer's day, there is a definite Mediterranean atmosphere along the coastal areas in the southwest, while on an overcast day you feel even further north than you are.

Steeped in legend and history, Ireland has cairns, stone circles, standing stones, ring-forts and countless burial sites, all testifying to diverse Neolithic cultures. These exciting archaeological finds will be special attractions on all your excursions. In the Middle Ages Ireland was a thriving land of saints, scholars and missionaries, when monasteries like Glendalough were important centres of learning. Many fine houses with beautiful landscaped gardens date from the period of English rule.

The richness of Ireland is not only reflected in its varied landscapes, myth-drenched sites and historic monuments, but also in its picturesque villages, lively towns and snug pubs where all the locals meet. You only begin to understand Ireland if you take refuge in a pub on a cold rainy day, contemplating life over a creamy Guinness or two, with the crackling turf fire giving off its unforgettable smell.

But most of all it is the people that really count. They really *are* friendlier, just as the grass *is* greener. The Irish are known for their hospitality, and rightly so — their boundless warmth will make you want to return again and again. However you like to spend your holidays, Ireland offers something for everybody. With the help of this book, you can easily escape the crowds and discover the Emerald Isle at its best. Although walking is emphasised, the book also features a good number of car tours that will take you on voyages of discovery. Travelling in Ireland is full of unexpected moments to be savoured, so take your time and explore at leisure.

Céad míle fáilte!

Recommended books

It should be emphasised that *Landscapes in Ireland* is a guide to countryside exploration and should be used in conjunction with standard guides. There are countless guidebooks covering Ireland in its entirety, but one of the best is the *Rough Guide to Ireland,* covering all aspects of the island. A wealth of information is also contained in the official *Ireland Guide* of Bord Fáilte. Also of interest is *Reading the Irish Landscape* by Frank Mitchell and Michael Ryan, published by TownHouse, Dublin, for its excellent account of the changing Irish landscape over the course of time.

White Strand, Beara Peninsula

Getting about

This is a countryside guide to *all* of Ireland, focusing on the mountainous coastal regions. Unless you have a great deal of time and are willing to hitch-hike occasionally (quite easy in the west), a **car** is certainly the most convenient way of getting around the country. Most visitors take their own cars anyway and come by ferry. If you come by air, you will find the usual international car hire firms at any of Ireland's airports. But if you are flying into one of the smaller airports, pre-booking is strongly recommended to ensure there is someone at the counter and a car in the desired category is available. Don't forget green card insurance cover if you are taking your own vehicle.

Petrol stations are numerous; even the most remote village will have one. The Republic has converted to the metric system, so all road signs (including speed limits) will be in kilometres, not miles.

From a walker's point of view, **public transport** is quite limited. Major towns and cities are well served, but the more remote countryside where you will want to walk is rarely reached by public transport. There are **trains** connecting the major cities, but unfortunately most local branches (including the scenic Galway to Clifden line) have long been closed. Even **buses** are rarely useful to the walker, since they stick to the main roads and don't take you to the starting points of most of the walks in this book. Most buses in the Republic are operated by Bus Éireann, while the North is mainly served by Ulsterbus.

Taxis could also be used, but are rather expensive.

All the inhabited islands off the coast can be reached by **boat.** Usually there are more frequent sailings in summer, as these islands are popular with visitors.

At the beginning of each walk I give transport details. The relevant timetables are on page 134, but please do not rely *solely* on these. Buy the complete up-to-date expressway and local bus timetable in a book-shop or at a kiosk; it's inexpensive and also includes the Ulsterbus Goldline Network. And remember, too: it always pays to verify departure *and return* times before setting out, and it's always a good idea to arrive early.

Picnicking

Official picnic sites offering a full range of facilities are surprisingly few in Ireland, and often, where they do exist, they are *too* accessible (just beside a main road for example). Picnic areas *with tables* are indicated both in the car touring notes and on the touring map by the symbol ⊼. Nevertheless, most coastal areas offer lovely picnic settings. The 29 suggestions below are all linked to the car tours and will take you to unspoilt locations where you can enjoy the tranquil mood of the country-side. All are within easy reach of the parking spots. Be careful where you park; *never* block a road or track. I advise common sense in your dress — that is, sturdy shoes for walking and adequate sun protection in the summer (○ indicates a picnic in full sun). It's a good idea to take along a plastic groundsheet as well, in case the ground is damp or prickly. *Please* take your litter away with you; sadly, enough bins are rarely provided.

All picnickers should read the country code on page 69 and go quietly in the countryside.

1a POWERSCOURT WATERFALL (touring map; photo page 15) ⊼

🚗 Car tour 1 at 50km/31mi; no walking.
Partly-wooded picnic area below the famous waterfall. WC; refreshments available in season.

1b POLLAPHUCA RESERVOIR (touring map) ⊼

🚗 Car tour 1 at 81km/51mi; no walking.
Lakeside setting near Three Castles, overlooking Pollaphuca Reservoir; some shade.

1c GLENDALOUGH (map pages 82-83; photos pages 16, 17-18, 79, 80-81, 83) ⊼

🚗 Follow Car tour 1 to the *second* car park at Glendalough (124km/77mi); no walking.
Beautiful parkland site with shady trees near the Upper Lake; can be busy on weekends. WC; information kiosk; refreshments in season.

2 TINTERN ABBEY (touring map; photographs pages 11, 20)

🚗 Car tour 2 at 27km/17mi; less than 5 minutes on foot. Park at the abbey and walk down the path to the old stone bridge.
You can picnic on the picturesque stone bridge or in the romantic old graveyard adjacent to the nearby chapel.

3a GLENAKEEFE RIVER (touring map) ⊼

🚗 Car tour 3 at 114km/71mi; no walking.
In a wooded coomb by the Glenakeefe River, a very peaceful spot that offers sun and shade — and the pleasant sound of running water.

3b CAHIR PARK (touring map; photo page 23)

🚗 Car tour 3 at 164km/102mi; no walking. From the car park cross the river Suir by the

wooden footbridge into the park.
*Overlooked by Cahir Castle, Cahir
Park on the banks of the Suir is a
lovely place to relax, with some
wooden benches to sit on. Welcome
shade under big oak trees on a hot
and sunny day. You could also
follow the riverside walk along the
east bank of the Suir.*

4a ST BRANDON'S CHURCH, CROOKHAVEN (touring map; photo page 27) ○

🚗 Car tour 4 at 185km/115mi;
no walking.
*Overlooking Crookhaven Bay and
surrounded by an old graveyard.
You can sit on the enclosing wall.
The only shade is from the church
wall.*

4b GOUGANE BARRA (touring map) 🌲

🚗 Optional detour on Car tour 4
(see page 29); no walking.
*Gougane Barra is a magnificent
mountain lake in a tranquil
setting. There are picnic spots in the
nearby forest park; plenty of shade.*

5a ILNACULLIN (touring map)

🚗 to Glengarriff, where Car tour
5 begins and ends. Leave your
transport in Glengarriff and take
the ⛴ to Ilnacullin (frequent
service); a few minutes on foot
to find a suitable spot.
*Bathed in the warm waters of the
Gulf Stream, Ilnacullin (or
Garinish Island) is a garden island
of exceptional beauty that supports a
luxuriant Mediterranean
vegetation. There are benches in the
gardens.*

5b DERREEN GARDENS (touring map)

🚗 Car tour 5 at 121km/75mi; a
few minutes on foot.
*This magnificent botanical garden
with its exotic plants and huge tree
ferns provides the peaceful setting
for a lovely picnic. No tables but
wooden benches to sit on. Shady
trees.*

5c GLEN INCHAQUIN (map page 92; photos pages 92-93) 🌲○

🚗 Car tour 5 at 141km/88mi.
No walking or 10 minutes on
foot. You can either picnic in the
designated area down by the
river below the waterfall or
follow Walk 6 in reverse for
about ten minutes to reach a
wooden table and bench
overlooking the entire valley.
*Glen Inchaquin is reminiscent of an
alpine valley. A waterfall tumbles
down the rock face, sheep graze
peacefully on the green grass, and
some scattered houses dot the slopes.*

5d GLENGARRIFF NATURE RESERVE (touring map) 🌲

🚗 Car tour 5 at 187km/116mi;
no walking.
*Shady picnic area close to a river in
the Glengarriff Nature Reserve.*

6a DINISH COTTAGE (map pages 96-97, photo page 95) 🌲

🚗 Car tour 6 at 13km/8.3mi; 25
minutes on foot. From the car
park/viewpoint follow the tarmac
lane to Dinish Cottage (Walk 7
in reverse).
*When there are few visitors about,
this is a very peaceful spot, overlooking the calm sheet of water.
Dinish Cottage is surrounded by
exotic plants, including eucalyptus,
Californian redwoods, and
camellias. You can sit on the
wooden benches and bring your own
food; during the season refreshments
are available. WC. Shade. Another
delightful spot is by the Meeting of
the Waters at the rear of the
cottage gardens, where the waters
from the Upper Lake divide to flow
round Dinish Island. Just
upstream, the picturesque Old Weir
Bridge arches over the rapids.*

6b LADIES' VIEW (touring map)

🚗 Car tour 6 at 22km/13mi; a
few minutes on foot.
This spectacular vantage point

affords commanding views over all the Killarney lakes. The mountainous backdrop to this splendid scenery is formed by Macgillycuddy's Reeks, rising majestically in the distance. You can sit on the smooth rocky outcrops overlooking the landscape. Little shade. Refreshments available in season. WC.

6c DERRYNANE (map page 107; photo page 107)

🚗 Car tour 6 at 81km/50mi; a few minutes on foot.
You can picnic anywhere in the Derrynane National Park — in the enchanting park where there are wooden benches, or on the nearby beach. Refreshments available in season. WC.

6d GLENCAR VALLEY (touring map) 🛱

🚗 Car tour 6 at 160km/99mi; no walking or 3 minutes on foot.
You can either picnic in the designated area or continue along the road for a few minutes to reach Blackstones Bridge which crosses the upper river Caragh. Here you can sit on boulders at the riverbank.

7 SLEA HEAD (touring map; photo pages 40-41) ○

🚗 Car tour 7 to the car park at Slea Head (see page 40), where there is an information board; it comes up just past a crucifix. No walking.
You can sit on the stone walls below the car park, with spectacular coastal views of the Blaskets.

8 CLIFFS OF MOHER (touring map; photograph page 46) ○

🚗 Car tour 8 at 23km/14mi; 10 minutes on foot. Leave your car in the car park and follow the footpath to O'Brien's Tower.
From this old watchtower, built in 1835 on a promontory, there is a spectacula view all along the cliffs. You can picnic near the tower. Some benches. Refreshments and WC facilities at the car park.

9 ALCOCK AND BROWN MONUMENT (touring map) ○

🚗 Car tour 9 at 112km/69mi; no walking.
Glorious panorama over the coastal region. Wooden benches.

10a KILGEEVER ABBEY (touring map) ○

🚗 Car tour 10 at 32km/20mi; 5 minutes on foot. Park in front of the new cemetery and walk down the track beside its wall to the abbey.
This ruined church, set in an old graveyard, is a very peaceful spot, but there is little shade.

10b ERREW ABBEY (touring map)

🚗 Car tour 10 at 107km/66mi; 10 minutes on foot. The road signposted to Errew Abbey ends in front of three iron gates, opposite a farm. Climb the stile by the right-hand gate and follow the line of maple trees to the right. Veer slightly left across the pasture, to a gap in the thicket on the far side. Beyond it Errew Abbey appears up to the right of the lake.
A ruined church peacefully situated on a small peninsula projecting into Lough Conn. Picnic at the church or anywhere by the lake.

11 CREEVELEA ABBEY (touring map; photo page 54)

🚗 Car tour 11 at 108km/67mi; or 🚌 no 462 or 469 from Sligo to Dromahair; 10 minutes on foot. From the signposted car park in the middle of Dromahair a footpath descends to the nearby Bonet River. Turn right after crossing the footbridge, to follow the pleasant riverside walk through a small wood and past a house to Creevelea Abbey.
The ruined Franciscan friary of Killanummery, popularly called Creevelea Abbey, is a tranquil spot that offers both sun and shade. You can sit on the stone walls or picnic in the wood beside the rushing river.

Old bridge at Tintern Abbey (Picnic 2; see also photograph page 20.)

12a GLENCOLUMBKILLE (touring map) 🚏○

🚗 Car tour 12 at 67km/42mi; no walking.
Excellent views over the peaceful Glencolumbkille glen.

12b GLENVEAGH NATIONAL PARK (touring map; photos page 61)

🚗 Car tour 12 at 283km/176mi; up to 5 minutes on foot. Leave your car at the car park near the visitors' centre. There is a regular minibus service between here and Glenveagh Castle.
Glenveagh Castle is surrounded by pleasant formal and informal gardens. WC; refreshments.

13a GLENARIFF FOREST PARK (touring map) 🚏

🚗 Car tour 13 at 28km/17mi; no walking.
Pleasant picnic area with barbecues, WC, refreshments. Sun or shade.

13b MURLOUGH BAY (touring map; photo page 64) ○

🚗 Car tour 13 at 68km/42mi; 10 minutes on foot. From the car park, follow the track ahead to the beach at the end of the bay.
Unspoilt sandy beach; no facilities and little shade.

13c THE GIANT'S CAUSEWAY (map page 131; photograph page 132) ○

🚗 Car tour 13 at 101km/63mi or 🚐 Ulsterbus no 172 from Ballycastle or Portrush to the Giant's Causeway; no walking or 15 minutes on foot. From the visitors' centre you can either walk down the tarmac lane to the Grand Causeway or take the frequent shuttle bus.
Picnic anywhere on the basalt columns that jut out into the sea. No facilities, but WC and refreshments at the visitors' centre.

14a STRUELL WELLS (touring map) 🚏

🚗 Car tour 14 at 59km/37mi; no walking.
Once a popular pilgrimage place, tranquil Struell Wells also makes a delightful picnic spot. The buildings comprise a ruined church, drinking well, eye well (holy water) and bathhouses in a lovely setting.

14b TOLLYMORE FOREST PARK (touring map) 🚏

🚗 Car tour 14 at 135km/84mi; no walking.
Picnic area with barbecues, restaurant, WC. Sun or shade.

Touring

In Ireland remote scenery can be enjoyed without even getting out of your car. Most tracks have been tarmacked over the past couple of decades — to the walker's regret but to the delight of motorists. Despite access by road, most places fortunately have preserved their feeling of wilderness. The mountainous southwest coast is the most popular corner of the island, with magnificent scenery not to be missed. However, progress along the Ring of Kerry and other popular routes in the southwest tends to be extremely slow in the main season. The 14 tours in this book cover the most scenic regions in Ireland. Each tour is designed to take in all the major sights in that particular area and to provide as much variety as possible.

If you are touring, consider spending the night en route, rather than trying to rush back to your base. When planning your tour, remember that you won't cover more than about 40km/25mi per hour on the narrow winding roads. Allow plenty of time for sight-seeing and stops at the many viewpoints. My driving times include only short breaks; most tours are too long to complete in one day if you drive at a speed leisurely enough to enjoy the scenery. Distances quoted are *cumulative km/miles* from the starting point.

Gaelic place names are given in *italics* and mostly translated — especially where they are still in use, mainly in the western *Gaeltachts* (Irish-speaking areas), where the country's ancient language has been preserved and many road signs are in Gaelic.

Drive carefully; even 'R' roads tend to be narrow and winding. Be aware also that roads almost invariably narrow appreciably where they cross bridges. **Petrol** stations are frequent and usually open seven days a week; there is one to be found in almost every village.

The touring notes are brief; they include little history or information about the towns and archaeological sites that is readily available in standard guide books; see the book list on page 6. I concentrate mainly on route-planning and the 'logistics' of touring: times and distances, facilities en route, viewpoints, and good places to rest. Most of all I emphasise possibilities for **walking**

12

and **picnicking** — all the walks and picnics in the book are highlighted, where relevant, in the car tours.

   The touring map is designed to be held out opposite the touring notes and contains all the information you will need to follow the suggested tours. Due to the small scale of this map only the major and relevant minor roads have been included. Lack of space prevents us from printing town plans, so I give you clear guidance through all built-up areas in the touring notes.

   The **symbols** used in the touring notes correspond to those on the pull-out map; see map key.

   All motorists should read the country code on pages 68-69 and go quietly in the countryside.

Dingle Harbour (Car tour 7)

Car tour 1: DUBLIN BEYOND THE PALE — THE WICKLOW MOUNTAINS

Wicklow • Roundwood • Powerscourt • Sally Gap • Blessington • Russborough House • Wicklow Gap • Glendalough • Laragh • Rathdrum • The Meeting of the Waters • Arklow • Brittas Bay • Wicklow

185km/115mi; 6h driving

En route: ⋒ at the Vale of Clara, Avondale House and Forest Park, Avonbeg River; Picnics (all with ⋒; see *P* symbol and pages 8-11): 1a-c; Walks: 1, 2, 3

All roads are in good condition.

K nown as the 'Garden of Ireland', county Wicklow extends just south of Dublin. This car tour takes you through its varied landscapes — from the flat east coast with its popular seaside resorts of Wicklow and Arklow to the Wicklow Mountains rising further inland. This granite massif consists of high rounded hilltops penetrated by steep-sided glens and wooded valleys. Among the highlights of this tour are Powerscourt Gardens and Waterfall (the highest in Ireland) and Glendalough, a valley famous for its unique natural beauty and for its historical and archaeological interest.

Leave the seaside resort and county town of **Wicklow** (*i* 🏔🏔🏠✕🏕⊕) by heading north on the main road (R750). Go straight through **Rathnew**, now following the N11. Immediately after crossing the Vartry River in **Ashford** (🏕), turn left on the R763 (sign 'Glendalough') and keep left at the fork soon encountered. Follow this small country lane past Devil's Glen Forest on the right. Keep right at another fork signposted for Glendalough and carry straight on through the shady wood, passing a forest road to the right. Emerging from the trees, continue ahead through pleasant countryside. When you come to a T-junction, turn right on the R755 to **Roundwood** (22km/14mi 🏠✕🏕).

Carry straight on along the main R755 towards Ennis-kerry, ignoring any forks to the right or left. Soon after leaving Roundwood behind, Vartry Reservoir appears on the right. Ignore the Sally Gap road to the left and keep ahead on the main road. Soon the distinctly-shaped Great Sugarloaf comes into view; the road runs straight over a windswept plain towards the western flank of the mountain. Pass a quarry on the right, follow the road downhill and watch for your sharp left turn (R760) to Enniskerry.

Follow the main road round to the right at a junction (straight ahead is the access road to Powerscourt Waterfall which you will be taking later). The road now takes you between neat stone walls through the wooded valley of the river Dargle. Immediately before reaching Enniskerry, the entrance gate to **Powerscourt**

George Barret's painting of Powerscourt Waterfall in the 1760s (now hanging in the National Gallery of Ireland) brought this beauty spot to the attention of tourists. The Dargle Valley below the falls is rich in wildlife, with oak trees, redwoods, beech, birch and rowan forming a natural habitat for many birds. You may also spot the white rumps of Sika deer. Native to Japan, they were introduced by Lord Powerscourt into the deer park he created in this valley in the 1800s.

Estate is on your left. Follow the fine avenue to the car park, for a visit to these famous gardens★ (42km/26mi ❀🔺✕). Powerscourt House (🏛) itself has been rebuilt, after being destroyed by fire in 1974.

To visit the famous waterfall, return the way you came for about 5km/3mi, to the signposted turn-off (now on your right). Follow this road straight across a small crossroads and turn left through the entrance gate at the next fork. A small tarmac road takes you to a car park opposite the spectacular **Powerscourt Waterfall**★ (50km/31mi ⊟WC*P*1a). Tumbling down over 120m/400ft, this is the highest falls in Ireland and a splendid picnic spot.

Return to the small crossroads and turn right to continue. Soon meet a T-junction and turn right again. The road runs alongside some rather dull conifer plantations on the right (several ⊟). Turn right when you meet the R759, following

a sign to Sally Gap. The road soon starts climbing through partly-reafforested hills, affording fantastic views (📷) to the left over the steep-sided glen drained by the Cloghoge River. Surrounded by precipitous slopes, Lough Tay is set at the bottom of the valley, while through a gap in the hills Lough Dan (photograph pages 84-85) is seen further downstream in the southwest. You pass two turn-offs on the left leading down into the glen (64km/40mi; closed to motorised traffic); park at the second turn-off, only 50m/yds past the first, for Walk 3.

The road gradually climbs towards the head of the valley. The small river running down the slope feeds the two lakes and is one of their main sources. By now the conifers have given way to bleak moorland. At the top of the rise you reach **Sally Gap** (70km/44mi) and cross the old military road that was built through the Wicklows around 1800. This exposed pass and

15

watershed leads straight over into the wide open valley of the river Liffey. Stay ahead and follow the road gradually downhill.

Meet a T-junction and turn left for Blessington, leaving the R759. Keep right at the next fork encountered, about half a mile later. When you draw level with the northern arm of Pollaphuca Reservoir on the left, you'll see a ruined fortified towerhouse by the roadside with some picnic tables and benches nearby (81km/51mi ⌷P1b). This is **Three Castles** (⌷) — or rather what is left of it. Continue along the road skirting the lake and pass a bridge on the left. Soon meet the N81 in **Blessington** (85km/53mi ✕▯) and turn left. Now watch carefully for the easily-missed turn-off on your right to Russborough House: it comes up some 4km/2.5mi beyond Blessington. Then take the first turn on your left to **Russborough House★** (90km/56mi ▯); it is a fine example of Georgian architecture and now houses an art collection.

Return to the N81, turn right and follow the main road past Pollaphuca Dam, until a signpost at a petrol station (▯ 'Glendalough, Hollywood, Wicklow Gap') diverts you off left on the R756. This road takes you through the hamlet of **Hollywood** before crossing the Kings River, a tributary of the river Liffey. The road continues through the valley along steep reafforested hillsides before reaching

Wicklow Gap (115km/71mi). Not far beyond this windy mountain pass, spectacular vistas open up on the right (▯). The road descends through the Vale of Glendasan to a junction where you turn right, soon reaching the first car park on the left at **Glendalough★** (*Gleann da Locha;* 'The Glen of the Two Lakes'; 122km/76mi ♣◉ ▯▯✕▲WC; Walk 1). Continue for another 1.6km/1mi to a second car park near the Upper Lake, the starting point for Walk 2 (♣▯⌷WCP1c). Even if you aren't walking, see pages 75 and 78-83 to make the most of your visit to the monastic buildings, the round tower and the lakes.

Return the way you came past the Wicklow Gap road and carry straight on to **Laragh** (127km/79mi *i*▮✕▯⌷), a small village pleasantly sited at

'Green road' at Glendalough; these old grassy trails make for some of the best walking in Ireland.

the juncture of several wooded glens. Turn right at the junction in the village on the R755 towards Rathdrum. A lovely drive through the beautiful Avonmore Valley follows. A shady oak wood (a rarity in Ireland) is encountered in a section of the valley called the Vale of Clara (129km/80mi; ⚲ on the left). The road takes you straight into **Rathdrum** (138kmi/86mi ✕🍴). Take a break in this quaint village (shown overleaf), and have a coffee at the central square. Go straight over the crossroads at the end of the village, following the signs to Avondale House. Leave this road where it bends to the right and drive straight ahead to **Avondale House and Forest Park** (140km/87mi 🏛⚲).

Leaving the estate through the entrance gate, turn left and drive to a crossroads where you turn right ('Parnell Drive'). Turn left at the next T-junction ('Parnell Drive, Avoca') and follow the R752 through the wooded valley of the Avonbeg River (⚲ on the left at 144km/89mi). Soon a sign announces **The Meeting of the Waters** (145km/90mi), where the Avonbeg and Avonmore join to form the Avoca River. The setting was immortalized by Thomas Moore, Ireland's national poet, in 1807. Follow the lush green Vale of Avoca downstream. It is particularly lovely in late spring, when the wild cherry trees are in full blossom. Keep right on the R752 at the next junction, ignoring the left turn to Avoca★ village. (But no doubt fans of *Ballykissangel* will want to take a detour into Avoca, where the TV series was filmed.) One of the many ruined churches belonging to the Church of Ireland now

Above: Upper Lake at Glendalough (Walk 2, Picnic 1c); left: pub at Rathdrum

about 0.5km/0.3mi after crossing the Avoca River and fork right on the R750 (just before reaching a Shell petrol station; ☎ — watch for a sign to the Arklow Bay Hotel). This road heads north along the east coast, affording glimpses of the Irish Sea. Your first access point to the long sandy beach of **Brittas Bay** comes up 10.1km/6.3mi along this road; there is a small car park on the left. A well-established footpath to the right leads through the dunes to the beach.

Continue on the R750 to reach Brittas Bay South Beach car park, soon followed by Brittas Bay North Beach. Watch for the signposted right turn to Silver Strand and take it, to stay on the R750. On the outskirts of Wicklow there is a car park on the right (☐) from where you can climb down to the coast before returning to **Wicklow** (185km/115mi).

appears on the right — quite an eerie sight on a misty day (150km/93mi ☃). Follow the main road round to the left at **Woodenbridge**, ignoring the right turn (☎; the wooden bridge has long given way to a more recent construction). You pass an unsightly chemical works on the left before entering **Arklow** (159km/99mi *i* ▲ ♦ ✕ ☎). Turn left at the roundabout and follow the N11 towards Wicklow. Leave the main road

Car tour 2: THE SOUTHEAST

**Wexford • Wellingtonbridge • Tintern Abbey • Ballyhack •
Waterford • Tramore • (Stradbally) • Dungarvan • Ardmore
• Youghal • Cork**

165km/102mi; 5h driving

En route: ⚲ near Annestown, Swan Lake; Picnic (see *P* symbol
and pages 8-11): 2

All roads are in good condition. See ferry details on page 134.

Ireland's southeastern coastline is a series of gentle
hills, rugged cliffs and narrow estuaries with some
lovely sand-fringed coves. Fine resorts, historic towns
and quaint old villages are some of the places visited on
this tour.

Leave **Wexford**
(*i*♰🛏▲✕🍽⊕M), an historic
town of narrow winding
streets, on the R733 to
Wellingtonbridge. The road
runs straight through flat fields
to **Wellingtonbridge**
(22km/14mi ✕🍽), where you
swing right across the
eponymous bridge, ignoring
the R736 to the left. Continue
on the R733 for 2.7km/1.7mi,
then turn left at a small
crossroads signposted 'Tintern
Abbey 2km'. When this
country lane veers left at a
junction, go straight ahead
through a gate flanked by stone
pillars and follow the gravel
road. Soon **Tintern Abbey**
appears down in the green flats
below (27km/17mi ♰🛏).
Founded circa 1200, this
former Cistercian abbey,
shown overleaf, was named
after Tintern Abbey in Wales,
from where its first monks
came. The building was later
converted into a private
residence and occupied until
the 1960s. From the abbey, a
footpath leads down the river
flats to a picturesque fortified
stone bridge with a romantic
old graveyard and chapel
nearby (*P*2; photograph page
11).
Return to the main R733 and

turn left to continue. Carry
straight on past any turnings
left or right. Descend through
Arthurstown, following the
signs 'Passage East/Car ferry'.
You enjoy beautiful views on
the left out over the estuary of
Waterford Harbour before
reaching **Ballyhack**
(39km/24mi 🛏✕🍽), from
where the ferry takes you
across the bay.
Drive through the old-world
village of **Passage East** on the
far shore, and follow the R683
to a T-junction. Turn right
towards Waterford and follow
the signs through the outskirts
into the city centre. Turn left
on the N25 at an intersection
with traffic lights and follow
the main road through
Waterford (48km/30mi
i🛏▲✕🍽⊕M). Situated on
the south bank of the Suir close
to the sea, this is the main
seaport in the southeast and a
major industrial city, perhaps
best known for its cut crystal.
Bear left at a Y-fork, taking the
R675 to **Tramore** (56km/
35mi *i*🛏▲✕🍽), a popular if
somewhat touristic resort with
a long sandy beach. Keep right
at the junction ('Fennor,
Dungarvan') at the end of the
village. Just before reaching the
hamlet of Annestown, there is

Tintern Abbey (Picnic 2) was founded just a few decades after the first Normans had landed at nearby Bannow Bay in 1169.

a car park on the left from where you could stride out along the coast. Beyond **Annestown**, more car parks with beautiful coastal views follow (⛱🏕). Stay ahead on the main R675 and ignore any turnings right or left. (You could however make an optional detour to Clonea Strand (🏔🏔⛱✕) by taking the signposted left turn for Stradbally. Cross the river Dulligan and turn left at a crossroads to reach the car park at this lovely sandy beach, a most inviting spot for a swim. This 24km/15mi return detour is not included in the distance readings.)

The main tour stays ahead on the R675 to reach the busy town of **Dungarvan** (78km/48mi *i*🏕🏔🏔⛱✕🏪⊕). Go through the market square and continue ahead on the N25 for Cork. After crossing the river Brickey, the road climbs into the partly-reafforested Drum Hills. Take the signposted left turn to Ardmore and follow the R673 through undulating country. **Ardmore** is a pretty village

with a long sandy beach (100km/62mi ☉🏔⛱✕🏪⊕). The R673 takes you back to the N25. Turn left and skirt the estuary formed by the river Blackwater to come into **Youghal★** (115km/71mi *i*🏕🏔🏔⛱✕🏪⊕). Follow the esplanade through the resort and stop for a stroll through this lovely historic town.

Stay on the N25 as you leave Youghal. **Castlemartyr** (133km/83mi ✕🏪) is a small village with a Carmelite monastery. Pass Swan Lake on the left (136km/84mi ⛱) before skirting Midleton. The N25 takes you into the outskirts of Cork. When the N8 joins from the north, just follow the signs into the city centre. **Cork★** (165km/ 102mi *i*🏕🏔🏔⛱✕🏪⊕M) is Ireland's third largest city and an important centre of industry and commerce. Crossed by many bridges, the river Lee flows in two main channels through the city.

Car tour 3: KILKENNY AND TIPPERARY — WHERE THE HEART OF IRELAND BEATS

Kilkenny • Kilmaganny • Carrick-on-Suir • Clonmel • Cappoquin • Lismore • The Vee • Clogheen • Mitchelstown Caves • Cahir • Knockgraffon Motte • Cashel

185km/115mi; 6h driving

En route: ⌁ in the Blackwater Valley, by the Glenakeefe River and near the Swiss Cottage; Picnics (see *P* symbol and pages 8-11): 3a-b

All roads are in good condition.

The area covered by this tour is a prosperous inland region where the counties of Tipperary, Kilkenny and Waterford meet. Its landscapes are extremely varied — rich plains, high mountains and lush river valleys. Lined by prosperous towns, the beautiful river Suir flows through a broad plain. Kilkenny is a lovely historic city situated on the banks of the river Nore. The whole area is steeped in history, boasting ancient round towers, monastic sites and ruined castles. Among the many important antiquities is the famous Rock of Cashel, for hundreds of years the seat of Munster kings.

The tour begins in the beautiful city of **Kilkenny★** (*Cill Choinnigh*; 'Canice's Church'; *i✝⊙▥ ▲▲▲✕⊊⊕*), with its narrow winding streets and fine old buildings. Head south and, when you meet the ring road, follow it to the roundabout with the signposted exit for Kells (the N76 is further west, the N10 further east). Head south on the R697 to **Kells** (14km/9mi ⊊), a small village reached after crossing the Kings River by Kells Bridge (note the old watermill downstream on the left). Turn left at the crossroads in Kells to reach the car park at **Kells Priory★** (✝). The extensive ruins of this fortified Augustinian monastery include the surrounding wall with its defensive towers.

Turn right opposite the car park and follow this country lane straight on to **Kilree Monastic Site** (17km/11mi ✝⊙). Set in a small grove on the right, it comprises a well-preserved round tower and a ruined church surrounded by old gravestones. Go straight over the next two crossroads. When you come to a T-junction, turn right on the R701. Stay on the R701 as it forks right soon after passing through **Newmarket** (23km/14mi); this turning is signposted 'Kilmaganee'. Straight ahead at this junction is a field track leading to nearby **Aghaviller Monastic Site** (✝⊙), another round tower and ruined church set in a wood.

Continue on the R701 to **Kilmaganny** (28km/18mi ⊊). Stay ahead in the village on the R697 joining from the right. Turn left at a T-junction, signposted to Carrick-on-Suir. The R697 runs through the woody upper reaches of the Lingaun Valley. Watch for a left turn signposted 'Kilkeeran Crosses' and follow this side road about 0.5km/0.3mi to the **Kilkieran High Crosses** on the right (38km/24mi ✝). Originally used as gathering places for prayers and sermons outside the church, two of the stone crosses have the typical 'Celtic' ringed heads and intricate ornamentation. There is also a holy well on the site. Return to the R697 and turn left to **Carrick-on-Suir** (*Carraig na Siuire*; 'The Rock of the Suir'; 45km/28mi ▉▲▲ ▲✕🍽⊕). Turn right at the first T-junction in town, follow the road round to the left and keep straight ahead at a crossroads with a set of traffic lights. Now follow the one-way-system; turn right at its end and then left across Dillon Bridge. Upstream you can see the lovely old bridge spanning the Suir. Turn right just beyond the bridge and right again at the next major junction, signposted to Rathgormuck. Now follow the main R680 ahead.

The road follows the most beautiful stretch of the river Suir, affording lovely views over the wide valley (📷). This section of the tour has it all ... shady woods and old stone walls, lush green pastures and fertile fields, stately homes and some ruined castles. Ignore any turnings as you approach Clonmel. Follow the main R680 round to the left across a small bridge opposite Tikincor Castle (instead of going straight across Sir Thomas Bridge spanning the Suir). Enter the outskirts of Clonmel and turn right at the first major crossroads for a visit to **Clonmel** (*Cluain Meala*; 'Honey Meadow'; 68km/42mi *i*✝▲▲▲✕🍽⊕M).

Return across one of the bridges to the main road on the south bank of the river, following signs for Youghal. Head west at a roundabout ('Nire scenic drive'). Soon turn left and follow the R671 south through the Kilmacomma Valley. Go straight over the crossroads at **Kilmanahan** (75km/47mi). Turn right at the next crossroads and right again at the following crossroads. **Newcastle** (84km/52mi 🍽) is pleasantly situated on the southern banks of the Suir beneath the Knockmealdown Mountains. At the junction, turn half left for Cappoquin. Notice a ruined church (✝) set in an old graveyard and the ivy-covered ruins of a riverside castle (▉), both on your right; then fork left almost immediately, following the sign for Mt Mellary.

This small country lane gradually climbs uphill into the Knockmealdown Mountains. (You reach a right turn where you could make a short detour of 1.6km/1mi return to Mount Melleray Monastery, founded by the Cistercians in 1831, when they were expelled from Brittany.) Continuing ahead, pass Melleray Grotto on the right immediately after crossing the Monavuuga River. When you meet a T-junction, turn left on the R669 to **Cappoquin** (*Ceapach Chuinn*; 'Conn's Plot of Land'; 103km/64mi ▲✕🍽), a quiet market town in the wooded Blackwater Valley. Go straight through the village, passing Cappoquin House (🏛) on the right.

Follow the N72 ahead through the beautiful Blackwater Valley (105km/65mi 🎐). Perched on a steep cliff on the opposite bank, Lismore Castle heralds your approach to Lismore, a heritage town well worth a visit. Note a right-hand turn signposted to Clogheen just before turning left across the bridge into town; this is your ongoing route after your visit to **Lismore** (*Lios Mór;* 'Great Enclosure'; 109km/68mi 🍴🏠✕🚻).

Now follow the Clogheen road (R668) up the woody Owennashad Valley. Leave this road just before it bends left across a bridge and continue ahead on a minor road through the wild and romantic coomb of the Glenakeefe River. Soon reach a car park on the left (114km/71mi 🅿); this lovely place by the riverside is a superb picnic spot off the beaten track (*P*3a). The road ascends as it leaves the glen before running dead straight across a plain. Ignore any side turnings until you rejoin the main R668, then turn right to continue.

Wild rhododendrons grace the roadside now, blooming lavishly in early summer. Bleak moorland begins to open up all around, with the Knockmealdown Mountains towering ahead. The R669 comes in from the right just before you cross Glentanagree Bridge. You pass a car park on the left affording a beautiful view (📷) over the Owennashad Valley and the reafforested slopes on the far side.

*Right: one of the Kilkieran High Crosses;
Below: Cahir Castle (Picnic 3b)*

Knockmealdown Gap, a wind-swept col flanked by steep mountainsides, marks the end of the ascent (123km/77mi 📷). At 340m/1115ft above sea level, this is the highest point in the car tour. In days long past, stagecoaches once changed horses at the old barrel-vaulted stone building by the roadside; there is also an altar up on the left dedicated to the Virgin. Down to the north a lush green plain opens up; this is where you are heading. As you descend the road, Bay Lough emerges on the slopes to the left. Soon reach **The Vee** (126km/79mi 📷), a superb vantage point on a sharp hairpin bend affording magnificent views out over the plain below.

Continue down to **Clogheen** (132km/82mi ✕🍴) and turn left at the T-junction to **Ballyporeen** (✕🍴). Turn right at the main junction in this village, following the sign to the Mitchelstown Caves. This narrow lane undulates through pleasant rural countryside. Watch for a sudden signposted turn on the left and follow it to a T-junction where you turn left again to the **Mitchelstown Caves★** (144km/90mi). There are two systems of limestone caves, both containing fantastic dripstone formations. The Old (or Desmond) Cave can only be entered by using a rope or ladder, but the New Cave can be visited comfortably on a guided tour.

Return to the last junction and keep straight ahead now, past your outward route, to cross the Coolagarranroe Bridge almost immediately. Reach the village of **Burncourt** and stay ahead past the first turning on the left. Fork half left when the road swings right, to reach the imposing ruins of **Burncourt House** (147km/92mi 🏛). Built around 1640, it is one of the finest gabled houses in Ireland in the Elizabethan-Jacobean style. It was burned down by Cromwell in 1650 (hence the name) and has remained in ruins ever since.

Return to Burncourt village, now taking the left turn signposted to Ballylooby. Turn left at a T-junction and pass a right turn that comes up almost at once. Ignoring all further turnings, come into **Ballylooby** (156km/97mi). Stay ahead on the R668 and follow this main road round to the left when you come to a crossroads. Meet a T-junction in **Cahir** (also called Caher; *Cathair;* 'Fortress') and turn right into the town centre. Cross the Suir and turn right immediately, to leave your car in the main car park by the castle (164km/102mi *i*🚻🏔⛰✕🍴⊕). Now explore the town leisurely on foot. Cahir Castle, an impressive structure by the riverside, has been fully restored and can be visited on guided tours. Cahir Park on the banks of the Suir south of the castle is a lovely place to relax (*P*3b).

Back in the car, continue to the market square and turn left for Cashel. (But for a detour to the Swiss Cottage, turn *right* instead, on the R670 signposted to Ardfinnan. Then fork right after 1.1km/0.7mi and follow this road through a pleasant wood (🏕) until it ends at a car park. A short footpath takes you down to the Suir and across a bridge to the Swiss Cottage★. Return the same way to Cahir. This detour

Near Cahir: the Swiss Cottage, a chalet-like 'cottage orné', was built in the early 19th century to a design by the Regency architect John Nash.

is 4km/2.5mi return.)
Leave Cahir on the R670 for Cashel and cross a bridge over the N8. Turn left almost at once (before joining the N8). Follow this road round to the left (there is a sign for Golden), where another road continues ahead. You pass **Knockgraffon Motte** (170km/106mi 🚶), a prominent mound commanding fine views over the fertile Suir Valley. It was reputedly the place were Munster kings were crowned, before Cashel rose to prominence. In later years the Anglo-Normans took over Knockgraffon and enlarged the *motte*. At the foot of the mound are the few remains of a ruined castle (🏚). When you meet a T-junction, turn right

for New Inn, soon passing another, more imposing ruined castle (🏚) on the right.
On coming to the N8, turn left for Cashel. The road runs through **New Inn** before continuing straight to **Cashel** (*Caiseal;* 'Stone Fort'; 185km/115mi *i* 🏔 🛏 ✕ 🎦 ⊕). Leave your car at one of the car parks to explore the town centre on foot. Cashel's main attraction is the famous Rock of Cashel★ just north of town, a prominent outcrop of limestone with a group of ecclesiastical buildings perched on top (♣◉). One of Ireland's most important historic sites, it was the seat of Munster kings from about 370 until 1101, when the rock was granted to the Church.

Car tour 4: WEST CORK — THE IRISH RIVIERA

Cork • Kinsale • Timoleague • Clonakilty • Castletownshend • Baltimore • Skibbereen • Schull • Mizen Head • Kilcrohane • Bantry • (Pass of Keimaneigh • Gougane Barra) • Glengarriff

278km/173mi; 9h driving

En route: ⚞ at Timoleague Abbey, Rinneen Forest, Lough Ine, Gougane Barra; Picnics (see **P** symbol and pages 8-11): 4a-b

All roads are in good condition.

This tour takes you along the magnificent coastline of Cork, the largest county in Ireland. You visit some historic towns and quaint old villages before reaching the country's most southwesterly peninsulas, jutting into the Atlantic — cliffs and headlands affording splendid views over the deeply-indented coastline. The warm waters of the Gulf Stream sustain a mild climate: exotic plants and trees abound in sheltered gardens, and on a sunny day there is a definite Mediterranean feel to these seascapes.

Leave **Cork★** (*Corcaigh*; 'Marshy Place'; *i*✝▲▲🛈✕🍽 ⊕**M**) by heading west on the N71* in the direction of Bandon. Cross the Owenboy River and reach a roundabout almost immediately. Take the second exit, the R607 signposted to Kinsale. Turn left at a T-junction and drive into **Kinsale** (*Cionn tSáile*; 'Tide Head'; 28km/18mi *i*▢▲▲🛈✕🍽**M**). Once one of the main ports of the British Navy, the town has preserved much of its old-world charm. Keep left on the main road at the junction in town and turn right in front of the harbour, following signs for Bandon and Garretstown. Leave Kinsale and soon turn left across a bridge to follow the Coast Road West R600. Keep right at the junction just beyond the bridge. When you reach a crossroads, turn left on the R604, to make

for a lovely beach. Swing right with the main R604 at a junction where the 'Scenic Route' continues ahead. Soon you pass **Garretstown Strand** on the left (41km/26mi). Fork left at the end of this long sandy beach and follow the road through Ballinspittle Forest, then turn left at a T-junction to rejoin the R600. Now keep ahead past any turnings. When you meet a T-junction, go left across the causeway. Turn left again immediately after crossing the Argidene River, to reach Timoleague Abbey (✝⚞WC), the impressive ruins of a 14th-century Franciscan friary at **Timoleague** (*Tigh Molaige*; 'House of Molaga'; 60km/ 37mi 🍽). Keep straight ahead at the junction past the abbey, ignoring the left turn across another causeway. Turn right into Timoleague (signposted for Clonakilty), and go left at the next T-junction, to rejoin the R600. Meet the N71 and turn left, soon reaching a roundabout. Turn right and follow the signs into

---

*If you first want to kiss the Blarney Stone, Blarney Castle is some 10km/6mi to the northwest, on the R617.

Clonakilty (*Cloich na Coillte;* 'O'Keelty's Clan'; 70km/43mi *i*✕🍴M).
Head west on the N71 to continue. After passing Ross Carbery off to the right, leave the N71 immediately by forking left on the R597 signposted to Glandore. Go over an old stone bridge across the Roury River and continue for 1.6km/1mi, before taking the signposted left turn for the Drumbeg Stone Circle. Fork right at another sign to reach the car park (88km/55mi). A footpath takes you past a kissing gate to the **Drumbeg Stone Circle** (🗿) — 17 evenly-placed standing stones dating from the Celtic era. Return to the main R597 and turn left. Pass through the peaceful little village of **Glandore** (90km/56mi 🏨🏠✕🍴), overlooking the waters of Glandore Harbour. Pass the pier on the left and keep left immediately, following the main road along the coast. Soon turn left across Poulgorm Bridge to **Unionhall** (🏨✕🍴), and turn right at a T-junction to pass through this quaint

village. When you come to a junction overlooked by a church on the left, keep right on the main road for Castletownshend. After passing through Rinneen Forest (🌲), keep left at a junction signposted to Skibbereen. Then turn left when you meet the main R595 at a crossroads, to visit the attractive village of **Castletownshend** (104km/65mi 🏨🏠✕🍴). Return on the R595 in the direction of Skibbereen. Pass the entrance to the **Liss Ard**

Drumbeg Stone Circle (top right), Glandore Harbour (right), and St Brandon's Church, Crookhaven (below; Picnic 4a)

Experience on the left (108km/67mi ❀), a landscaped garden in contemporary style, designed to stimulate awareness of Ireland's natural history and environment . At a crossroads on the outskirts of Skibbereen, turn left to continue on the R595. Take the signposted left turn to **Lough Ine** (or Hyne; 115km/72mi ⊼), a landlocked inlet enclosed by wooded hillsides. Turn right alongside the shore, then keep right at a junction to leave the lake. Turn left at the next junction, and right again at the following junction. Now ignore any turnings until you meet the main R595, where you go left into the fishing village of **Baltimore** (122km/76mi ⌂✕❮▮). Return on the R595 to the crossroads on the outskirts of Skibbereen that you passed earlier and turn left. Reach the town centre of **Skibbereen** (*Sciobairín;* 'Little Boat Harbour'; 135km/84mi *i*⌂✕❮), where you turn left onto the N71 heading west. Cross the river Ilen and keep left at a junction, on the N71 for Ballydehob. Leave the N71 when it bends right, and go ahead across a bridge into **Ballydehob** (*Béal an dhá Chab;* 'Ford at the Mouth of Two Rivers'; 150km/93mi ✕❮). Note the bridge with twelve arches, on the left, just before entering the village — a remnant of the old West Cork railway system.

Keep right at the junction in the village and continue on the main R592, past mushroom-topped Mount Gabriel on the right, to **Schull** (or Skull; 158km/98mi ⌂✕❮). Keep right on the R592 when the road forks at the end of this pleasant village. The road sweeps round Toormore Bay, past a church on the right and the R591 off to the right. At the end of **Goleen** (164km/102mi ✕❮), opposite a church, take a right turn signposted to Mizen Head. Follow this road straight ahead past a left turn to Crookhaven (you'll be taking this road on your way back). Take the next turn on the left and follow the road until it ends at **Mizen Head★** (175km/109mi), Ireland's most southwesterly point. Mizen Head Signal Fog Station, with the famous bridge (📷) shown opposite, is open to the public.

Return the same way to the junction passed earlier and turn right across the causeway to Crookhaven. Soon you enjoy a fine view on the right (📷) over Barley Cove with its golden sandy beach. Keep right at the junction opposite the next bay (Crook Haven). Ignore a right turn to Brow Head and follow the R591 into **Crookhaven** (185km/115mi). At the entrance to this sleepy little fishing village you'll find St Brandon's Church (*P*4a) on the left. It overlooks the bay and its sheltered harbour, which is popular with yachting enthusiasts.

Return to the junction passed earlier, now keeping right on the R591 for Goleen. You enjoy lovely views across the bay to Crookhaven before reaching Goleen again. Drive back in the direction of Schull for a short distance, then turn left at Toormore Bay on the R591 to Bantry. Dunmanus Bay comes into view on the left. At **Durrus** (227km/141mi ❮) take a sharp left turn

The suspension bridge at Mizen Head was one of the first reinforced concrete structures in Europe, built between 1908 and 1910.

towards Kilcrohane. This coast road runs along the northern shore of Dunmanus Bay to **Kilcrohane** (243km/151mi 🚉), peacefully situated on the Sheep's Head peninsula. Turn right at the village church, following the sign 'Goats Path', and wind your way up the hill. You cross a saddle on the ridge (👁), with beautiful views over Dunmanus Bay to the south and Bantry Bay to the north. Follow the main road along the northern side of Sheep's Head, ignoring any turnings. You are heading east through a rather desolate and wind-swept countryside; some whitewashed houses dot the landscape. Meet the N71 and turn left to **Bantry** (*Beanntraí*; 'Descendants of Beann'; 267km/166mi *i* 🏨 🛏 ✕ 🚉). Bantry House and Gardens (🏛✿) definitely merit a visit; the entrance is on the right just as you enter the town.

(Not far beyond Bantry you could make a detour of 50km/30mi return into the Shehy Mountains. This comes up immediately after crossing the Owvane River: turn right on the R584 signposted to Gougane Barra. Follow the scenic R584 through the wide Owvane Valley, keeping left at a fork for Macroom. Cross the Carriganass Bridge and follow the course of the Owvane, now on your right. The road gradually climbs through a gorge-like gap called the Pass of Keimaneigh ('Deer's Pass') into the Shehy range. As the ascent eases, watch for the left turn to Gougane Barra★ — a magnificent mountain lake in a tranquil setting (♨✕WC). On the tiny island in the lake stands a chapel where St Finbarr, patron saint of Cork, once had his hermitage. Continue left alongside the shore of the lake, to reach a shady forest park (🎪P4b) where some lovely nature trails have been waymarked.)

The main tour follows the N71 straight on to **Glengarriff** (*Gleann Garbh*; 'Rugged Glen'; 278km/173mi *i* 🏨 🛏 ✕ 🚉), where you could link up with Car tour 5.

Car tour 5: THE RING OF BEARA

Glengarriff • Castletown-Bearhaven • (Bear Island) • Dunboy Castle • Dursey Sound • Allihies • Eyeries • Ardgroom • Lauragh • Derreen Gardens • Kenmare • Glengarriff Nature Reserve • Glengarriff

191km/119mi; 6h driving

En route: ⊼ at the Lehanore Ring fort; Picnics (see **P** symbol and pages 8-11): 5a-b and 5c-d with ⊼; Walks: 4, 5, 6

All roads are in good condition, but some lanes are narrow and winding.

O ne of the long peninsulas in Ireland's southwest, the Beara projects for over 50km (30 miles) into the Atlantic. The rocky Caha and Slieve Miskish ranges form the mountainous backbone of the peninsula that is famous for its magnificent unspoilt natural beauty. This tour does *not* follow the 'official' Ring of Beara route, so ignore the signs and use the touring notes instead.

Start out at **Glengarriff** (*Gleann Garbh;* 'Rugged Glen'; *i* 🏔🏔🛏✕🎥), a pleasant holiday resort surrounded by thickly-wooded hillsides at the head of Glengarriff Harbour. The entrance to the estuary is guarded by the island of Ilnacullin★ (or Garinish Island). Bathed in the warm waters of the Gulf Stream, it is a garden island of exceptional beauty that supports a luxuriant Mediterranean vegetation. Ilnacullin can easily be reached by boat from Glengarriff and is definitely worth the trip (❀*P*5a).

Fork left at the main junction in Glengarriff on the R572 for Castletown-Bearhaven. This road out onto the Beara Peninsula skirts Bantry Bay and follows the rocky coastal strip beneath the Caha Mountains, with Sugarloaf Mountain rising prominently on your right. Turn left after crossing the Adrigole Bridge (18km/11mi) and continue along the coast to **Castletown-Bearhaven** (34km/21mi 🛏✕🎥). To get to

Walk 5 on Bear Island (photograph page 34), leave your car at the harbour opposite the Eyeries road and take the ferry. Between the island and the mainland lies the sheltered port of Bear Haven, where Dreadnought battleships of the British Navy were moored until 1938. Continuing ahead on the R572, soon take a signposted turn on the left for a short foray to **Dunboy Castle** (37km/23mi ∎). Then follow the R572 along the coastal strip beneath the Slieve Miskish Mountains. Turn left at the signposted junction for the Dursey cable car, thus staying on the R572 (straight ahead is the R575 to Allihies). There is a stile on the left and a sign 'Wegde Grave' at this turning. You can see this megalithic tomb or dolmen (⏏) down in the meadow close to an electricity pole. Pass a lay-by on the left (⊼) and note a sign for the Lehanore Ring Fort (⏏) after another 0.15km/0.1mi. This prehistoric

Eyeries — where even the cars are colour-coordinated with the houses

enclosure down on the hillside to the left is in a strategic position overlooking the sea. Follow the main road through the steep-sided Firkeel Gap until it ends at **Dursey Sound** (59km/37mi 📷). A cable car operates across the sound to Dursey Island opposite.

Now return to the junction passed earlier and turn left on the R575 for Allihies. Just beyond Bealbarnish Gap, a lay-by on the right affords the glorious views (📷) shown overleaf — out over the seascape around Allihies Point and the Slieve Miskish Mountains rising inland. When you reach a three-way junction, you could turn left to make a short detour to Ballydonegan Beach (WC). Pass through **Allihies** (72km/45mi ✕🍺; Walk 4) and keep left for Eyeries when the road forks at the end of the village. After about 1.6km/1mi you could stop at a lay-by, to see the eerie ruins of the old copper mines (one of which is shown on page 89). But view them from a safe distance; don't venture into the hills — the old

mineshafts are liable to subsidence. Have a close look at the stones by the roadside here, too; if you are lucky you'll not only find red iron ores, but also pieces containing greenish copper oxides.

The road continues to snake up and down through the hills; driving along this winding roller-coaster route you are bound to loose your sense of orientation. There is a sign-posted 'mass rock' on the right shortly before you swing round to the right on the main road through **Cahirkeen**. Cross the Kealincha River by the Drehidawillaun Bridge and keep left at the junction just beyond it. On meeting the main R571 almost at once, turn left towards Eyeries. Reach a junction at the entrance to the village and keep left, following 'Ring of Beara', to pass through **Eyeries** (89km/55mi ✕🍺) with its colourful houses.

Keep left at a junction ('Ring of Beara') and notice the standing stone on the left almost immediately. Take the next left turn across a bridge to

31

visit **Ballycrovane Ogham
Stone★**, the largest of its kind.
A signposted footpath leads
past a cottage, where you pay
admission to see this standing
stone (shown overleaf). Then
return to the bridge and turn
left to continue on the coast
road as it winds up and down
through the rocky landscape.
Pass Kilcatherine on the right,
a ruined church with an old
graveyard (⚲). Derryvegal
Lough appears down on the
left, and then the inlet of
Cleanderry Harbour with its
mussel beds opens up before
you. Keep left at a junction,
still following the Ring of
Beara. Keep left again at a
signposted junction, to follow
the coast road to the pier at
Pallas Harbour, another inlet
with mussel beds.
Skirt Ardgroom Harbour and
cross Cappul Bridge to come
into **Ardgroom** (109km/68mi
✗📷). At the petrol station,

turn left on the R571. Now
Kilmakilloge Harbour with its
mussel beds opens up before
you. A sign on the right
pointing to the Cashelkeelty
stone circle gives you an
opportunity to stretch your
legs, so leave your car by the
roadside and follow the
footpath to this megalithic
monument dating from the
Celtic era.
Continuing the tour, soon
cross Croanshagh Bridge and
pass the quaint **Lauragh** post
office on your right
(120km/74mi). Fork left on
the R573 after 0.8km/0.5mi
and, after another
0.25km/0.15mi, watch for the
sudden left turn to **Derreen
Gardens** (121km/75mi
❀*P*5b), a magnificent botanical
garden with exotic plants and
huge tree ferns.
Continuing on the R573, pass
the lovely Keeper's Cottage on
the right. Proceed along the

main coast road past **Kilmakilloge Pier** (125km/78mi). You pass a crucifix on the right at **Tuosist** shortly before meeting a T-junction, where you turn left on the R571 for Kenmare. Lower Cloonee Lough soon comes into view on the right just before you cross Ardea Bridge over the Cloonee River. Now watch for a right turn that comes up after 1.4km/ 0.9mi, signposted 'Inchiquin Lake, Waterfall, Uragh Stone Circle'. Follow this small tarmac lane past the Middle and Upper Cloonee Lough, hidden on your right. Ignore a track to the right, signposted to the Uragh Stone Circle (**ᴨ**), and continue along the tarmac lane to Lough Inchaquin by keeping right at a fork near the shore. The road ends at the last house in the valley (141km/88mi ⌂*P*5c). **Glen Inchaquin**, shown on pages 92-93, is reminiscent of an alpine valley. A waterfall tumbles down the rock face at the head of the glen, sheep graze peacefully in the green valley, and some scattered houses dot the slopes. Walk 6 begins and ends here.

Return the same way to the main R571 and turn right, passing some fine estates with huge laurels, camellias and dragon trees. When you meet a T-junction, turn left on the N71 and cross the bridge into **Kenmare** (*Neidín;* 'Little Nest'; 160km/99mi *i* ⛰ ⌂ ✕ ☕), a charming town with pleasant old houses and a Celtic stone circle (**ᴨ**).

Leave Kenmare the way you came in, heading south on the N71 across the bridge that takes you over the Kenmare River. Stay ahead on this road as it follows the Sheen Valley, before cutting across a desolate mountain chain through a series of tunnels. When the road begins to descend, take the signposted right turn to Barley Lake; it comes up some 0.65km/0.4mi after leaving the last tunnel. Descend this narrow road steeply downhill and follow it round to the right (where a track continues ahead). At the next junction, in front of a house, keep left. On reaching a T-junction, turn left for 'Barley Lake, Glengarriff'. At the next junction, turn right across a bridge, following 'Barley Lake' (you'll take a left here on your way back). Climb the main road through a scattering of houses. The ascent steepens after you leave the last house behind, and you

The Beara Peninsula, with the Slieve Miskish Mountains rising in the distance

Above left: lighthouse on Bear Island (Walk 5); left: cut turf above Barley Lake; above right: Bally-crovane Ogham Stone. Before the introduction of Latin around the 5th century, the Celtic line-based writing system known as ogham was in use and can be seen inscribed on ancient standing stones.

begin to rise in a series of hairpin bends. There are fine views to the north, out over the steep-sided Kerry Valley. Leave your car at the end of the road on Crossterry Mountain (184km/114mi) and follow the path ahead for a few minutes to enjoy the view down over **Barley Lake** (📷), set in a remote mountain wilderness.

Return the same way you came, recrossing the bridge in the valley, and turn right just beyond it for Glengarriff. The road winds through the lovely valley, thickly wooded with grand old oak trees, elms, yews and holly. This is the

Glengarriff Nature Reserve; for short walk suggestions in this area contact the local tourist information. Keep left at a junction, soon passing a forest picnic area on the right by the side of the river (187km/116mi ⊐P5d). Cross a small stone bridge over the Canrooska River and ignore the track to the right not far beyond it. When you meet the N71, turn right, completing the Ring of Beara by heading back into **Glengarriff** (191km/119mi).

Car tour 6: THE RING OF KERRY

Killarney • Muckross House and Gardens • Ladies' View • Moll's Gap • Sneem • Staigue Fort • Derrynane National Historic Park • Coomakesta Pass • Waterville • Cahirciveen • Glenbeigh • Lough Caragh • Glencar • Beaufort • Killarney

194km/120mi; 6h driving

En route: ⊼ at Five Mile Bridge, Rossbeigh Strand; Picnics (see **P** symbol and pages 8-11): 6a and 6d with ⊼, 6b-c; Walks: 7-11

All main roads are in good condition, but some minor roads are narrow and winding. Some bad potholes between Lough Caragh and Beaufort.

Kerry is a perfect blend of mountain and sea, wooded glens and sandy beaches, luxuriant woodland and bleak bog ... there is something to suit every taste. This tour follows the famous Ring of Kerry, a scenic route along the coastal strip around the Iveragh Peninsula (or Waterville Promontory, as it is sometimes called), the largest peninsula in the southwest. We also take in some wild mountain scenery well off the beaten track, where Macgillycuddy's Reeks, the highest mountains in Ireland, loom majestically in the background. Beautiful Killarney, in the Kerry heartland, surrounded by lakes and mountains, is the ideal base for exploring the Iveragh Peninsula.

From the lively town of **Killarney** (*Cill Airne*; 'Church of the Sloe'; *i* 🏨🏨🛏✕🖰⊕) head south on the N71, following signs for Ross Castle and Muckross. Just before a petrol station on the right, take the signposted right turn to **Ross Castle** (2.9km/1.8mi ▢WC), a restored fortification overlooking Ross Bay. Jaunting cars (photograph page 95) and boats are for hire near the car park; the boat trip across the Killarney lakes to Lord Brandon's Cottage (Walk 8) is most enjoyable. Return to the main N71 and turn right. Walk 7 starts at the first signposted car park on your right. After another 1km/0.6mi, turn right to **Muckross House and Gardens** (🏛🏚WC), the beautiful estate shown on page 102. The main road then takes you through **Killarney National Park★** — the luxuriant woodlands around Killarney's lake district. Pass a car park on the left near the **Torc Waterfall** (12km/7mi WC; photograph page 97), another possible starting point for Walk 7. The waterfall itself is reached by a short footpath that ascends through a lovely wooded glen. Its waters tumble down over a series of sandstone crags more than 20m/60ft high. On resuming the journey, the road passes beneath densely-wooded Torc Mountain, to skirt Muckross Lake on the right. You reach another car park on the right (13km/8mi), where Walk 7 crosses the road. A short distance from here is lovely Dinish Cottage on Dinish Island (**P**6a). Leaving the lake behind, the road gradually winds up the

35

hill. You cross Five Mile Bridge (16km/10mi 🍴); down to the right there is a stretch of water called The Long Range. Soon you pass through a short tunnel cut into the rock. The road winds its way through a rocky landscape as the Upper Lake comes into view on the right. Pass a castle-like ruin on the left shortly before reaching **Ladies' View** (22km/13mi 📷), a spectacular vantage point affording commanding views over all the Killarney lakes. The mountainous backdrop to this splendid scenery is formed by Macgillycuddy's

Reeks (photograph page 104) rising majestically in the distance. The smooth rocky outcrops overlooking the landscape make a perfect picnic spot (**P**6b).

The road then passes Looscaunagh Lough on the left before reaching a junction at **Moll's Gap** with its popular restaurant (28km/17mi ✕). Turn right on the R568 for Sneem. Keep left on the main road at the next junction. Soon Barfinnihy Lough comes into view on the right. Not long after, far-reaching vistas over open hill country begin to unfold on the left. Continue ahead past any turnings, but keep right at an *unmarked* Y-fork to stay on the R568.

On meeting the N70 in **Sneem** (*An Snaidhm*; 'The Knot'; 51km/32mi 🛏✕📷), turn right to continue. You have now

Left: Lough Leane (Walks 7 and 8); below: Iveragh Peninsula

joined the official Ring of Kerry — as you can tell by the wearisome volume of traffic. Soon you enjoy beautiful views over the estuary of the Kenmare River backed by the Beara Peninsula. Pass through the small village of **Castle Cove** (*An Siopa Dubh;* 64km/40mi ⛽) and turn right on a minor road some 0.2km/0.1m beyond the post office (signposted to the Staigue Fort). Keep right at the first junction, but turn left at the next one. A sign on the right alerts you to an old arched stone bridge. You reach a large car park at the end of the road (68km/42mi). On the hillock to the right, across the valley, is the imposing **Staigue Fort** (ΠΓ), one of the most famous and best-preserved Celtic ring forts.

Return to the N70 and turn right to continue. Your next foray off the main road is in the village of **Cahirdaniel**

(*Cathair Dónall*), where you turn left to Derrynane House. Pass an ogham stone (ΠΓ) on the left and keep left at the following junction, to reach **Derrynane National Historic Park** (81km/50mi 🏛❀WC*P*6c; Walk 10). There is an interesting nature trail here, and a beautiful sand-fringed cove nearby (see photograph and text overleaf).

Return to Cahirdaniel and turn left to rejoin the Ring of Kerry. As the road rises and crosses the **Coomakesta Pass** (89km/55mi 📷), stop at the car park on the left, overlooked by a statue of the Virgin, to enjoy a magnificent view of Ballinskelligs Bay. Beyond the pass, the road winds down to **Waterville** (*An Coireán;* 'The Little Whirlpool'; 97km/60mi ▲▲▲✕⛽). Park here for circular Walk 11 round Lough Currane. Continue along the main road to **Cahirciveen** (*Cathair Saidhbhin;* 'Stone Fort of Sabina'; 113km/70mi *i*▲✕⛽). The Ring of Kerry now proceeds through a wide valley to **Kells**, where it runs close to the coast. Beyond the village the corniche runs high above the sea along precipitous slopes, affording a splendid outlook over Dingle Bay (📷). **Glenbeigh** (*Gleann Beithe;* 'Birch Glen'; 141km/87mi ▲✕⛽) is a small holiday resort near Rossbehy Point. Take a sharp left turn opposite the Church of Ireland for a short side-trip to Rossbeigh Strand. This takes you to a car park at the beginning of a long sandy beach backed by dunes projecting into Dingle Bay (⛩WC).

From Glenbeigh continue on the N70, to cross the Caragh. Just 1.6km/1mi beyond the

Ross Castle and Muckross Lake

bridge, leave the N70 and fork right on a minor road signposted to Caragh Lake. Take the next right turn *(not signposted)*, soon re-crossing the Caragh. Now stay ahead on the road that skirts the western side of **Lough Caragh** and ignore any turnings. Note a yellow house on the left and a picnic site on the right some 0.3km/0.2mi before reaching Blackstones Bridge which crosses the upper Caragh (160km/99mi ***P***6d).

Cross Blackstones Bridge (▲) and keep right at a junction 1.6km/1mi further on. Soon reach **Glencar** (163km/101mi ▲▲✕), a small scattering of houses with a post office and telephone box in the centre. Carry straight on past a sharp right turn. Before long, isolated Lough Acoose appears down on the right, set in the midst of wild hill country. Past the lake, a pleasant valley opens up on your left. Keep right at a junction for 'Beaufort, Killarney, Gap of Dunloe'. Turn right again at the next junction ('Gap of Dunloe 15km'). Now continue ahead past any turnings, with Macgillycuddy's Reeks towering on the right. Pass a right turn and cross the Gaddagh River immediately. (Note a sharp right turn signposted to Cronin's Yard 1.5km/0.9mi beyond the bridge; this detour would take you up to the starting point for Walk 9, shown on page 104.)

Continue ahead to cross another bridge almost at once, and go straight over a crossroads (⛽). Winding through the countryside past occasional houses, the road leads to a staggered intersection. (A detour to the right would take you to Kate Kearney's Cottage (✕) at the beginning of the Gap of Dunloe★ (⛽WC); allow 3km/1.9mi return.)

The main tour turns left to Beaufort here. Keep left at a junction, to cross an old stone bridge. Pass through **Beaufort** (184km/115mi ▲) and cross the Laune on the old Beaufort Bridge. Rejoin the N72 (⛽) and turn right. Take a sharp left turn after 3.2km/2mi, then fork right at the next junction, to reach **Aghadoe Church and Round Tower** (190km/118mi ✝◉). There is a marvellous view south over Lough Leane from up here. Fork right at the church and descend the hillside to rejoin the N72. Turn left and return to **Killarney** (194km/120mi).

Car tour 7: THE DINGLE PENINSULA

Castlemaine • Inch Strand • Anascaul • Dingle • Slea Head • Dunquin • Ballyferriter • Dingle • Connor Pass • Brandon Point • Castlegregory • Tralee

186km/116mi; 6h driving

En route: ⊞ at Slea Head and near the Connor Pass; Picnic (see *P* symbol and pages 8-11): 7; Walks: 12, 13

All roads are in good condition, except for some narrow and winding sections in the western part of the peninsula.

The Dingle Peninsula is the most northerly of the hilly promontories projecting into the Atlantic in Ireland's southwest. Wild hills build up the mountainous backbone of the peninsula, while the fertile coastal strip is studded with typical Irish villages. Steep cliffs and golden beaches alternate along the splendid coastline. This tour features spectacular seascapes and mighty mountains, including the majestic rampart of Brandon, the second-highest summit in the country. The Dingle Peninsula belongs to the Gaeltachts where Irish is still spoken and traditional lore is very much alive, so be prepared to encounter quite a few road signs in Gaelic.

Take the exit for Inch Strand at the roundabout in the centre of **Castlemaine** (⚑✕🅿). The R561 runs dead straight over the flat coastal strip of the Dingle Peninsula, with the Slieve Mish Mountains towering on the right. Across the almost land-locked harbour of Castlemaine to the left, Macgillycuddy's Reeks can be seen in the distance. A short way beyond the small seaside resort of **Inch** (⚑✕🅿), take the left turn to **Inch Strand** (20km/12mi). Enjoy a stroll along this sandhill spit fringed by a magnificent beach of golden sand.

The coast road continues along Red Cliff before swinging inland. Keep right at a Y-fork and turn right again at the next T-junction. Pass the left turn to Anascaul Lake (Walk 12; photograph page 112) and cross the Owenascaul River, to come into the quaint village of

Anascaul (*Abhainn an Scáil*; 28km/17mi ⚑✕🅿). Leave Anascaul the way you came, and turn left again at the end of the village soon after the bridge. Ignore the sharp right turn back to the N86, but fork right on a small country lane some 0.2km/0.12mi beyond it. You reach a lovely unspoilt cove with a sandy beach backed by boulders and overlooked by **Minard Castle** (*Caisleán Na Minairde*; 33km/21mi 🏚) — a stronghold said to have been destroyed in the very first attack!

The road swings right below the castle, and you soon reach a junction: turn right. Continue ahead past some houses and ignore any turn-offs until you meet a T-junction in **Bheag** (*An Bhánóg*). Turn left to **Lispole** (*Lios Póil*; 🅿). Keep straight on in this village, to join the main N86. Notice the imposing *Araucaria* (monkey-

39

The Blasket Islands from the summit of Mt Eagle (Walk 13)

puzzle tree) on the left, a particularly fine specimen. Turn left at the roundabout in **Dingle** (*An Daingean;* 'The Fortress'; 47km/29mi 🛏🗙📷) and left again at the next T-junction. Dingle Harbour (WC; photograph page 13) and the main car park are on your left. Explore the pretty town on foot.

Continuing along the road, turn left at an intersection across old Milltown Bridge, following signs for Slea Head Drive. Pass a right turn in **Milltown** almost immediately and follow the R559 straight ahead. Leaving Dingle Harbour behind, Ventry Harbour comes into view on the left, with the rounded hilltop of Mount Eagle beyond it. After passing through the small village of **Ventry** (*Ceann Trá;* 54km/34mi 🛏🗙📷), go straight over the first crossroads (⛧), to continue circling Ventry Harbour. Turn right at the next crossroads and stay on the main road (or make a short detour to the left to the sandy beach at Ventry Harbour).

Continuing on the main R559, follow the corniche round **Slea Head**, along the steep southwestern slopes of Mount Eagle (📷). The seascapes are spectacular, with splendid views across Dingle Bay to the Iveragh Peninsula and out to the Blasket Islands. This group, the most westerly off the Irish coast, comprises seven sizeable islands and isolated rocks. While Great Blasket is the biggest, Inishtooskert is the most prominent — its outline justifiably giving rise to the

name 'Dead Man Island'. For a picnic overlooking the Blaskets, stop at the car park where there is an information board (**P7**); it comes shortly after passing a crucifix. (Two short detours are possible here. The first would take you to a sandy cove: take the next sharp left turn, signposted 'Trá Choum Uí Neoil', to a car park with 🟥. A second possibility is a visit to Great Blasket — only possible in high season. To get there, take a left turn at the next right-hand bend, following the sign to Dunquin (*Cé Dhún Chaoin*). Leave your car at the car park and walk down to Dunquin Pier for the boat.)

The main tour continues on the R559 through the scattered houses of **Dunquin**. (Access to Walk 13 involves another detour here: on coming to a left-hand bend in the road, turn right on a narrow road

signposted to *Ceann Trá* (Ventry). About 0.9km/0.6mi up this road, turn right on a track and park at the side. This detour is not included in the distance readings.) Continuing on the main R559, soon reach a signposted crossroads where a short side-trip to the left takes you to The Great Blasket Centre (**M**).

Superb views unfold as you round a bend to the right, with the broad inlet of Smerwick Harbour opening up before you. A promontory rises to the left, extending from Sybil Point to The Three Sisters, spectacular cliffs. Brandon Mountain in the east forms the majestic backdrop to this dramatic coastal scenery. Keep ahead on the main R559. You pass through the small village of **Ballyferriter** (*Baile an Fheirtéaraigh*; 78km/48mi ⌂✗☎M). Follow the main road round a sharp left turn

('Slea Head Drive') and soon keep left again at a junction, for a short foray to Wine Strand (*Tráigh an Fhíona*). You pass through a scattering of houses and come to a small headland projecting into Smerwick Harbour. A sandy beach stretches to the left along this beautiful sheltered bay. Then return to the main R559 and turn left. Take the left turn signposted to 'Slea Head Drive, An Mhuiríoch' that comes after 2km/1.2mi. Fork right at the next bend to the left, to visit **Gallarus Oratory★** (⌘), one of the best-preserved early Christian churches in Ireland. Of drystone construction, it is over 1000 years old. Return to the main road and continue straight ahead. Keep right at the junction in **Murreagh** (*An Mhuiríoch*; 88km/55mi ⌂✗), then fork right almost immediately, following the

41

Top left: ring fort near Kilmalkedar Church; left: Gallarus Oratory; top right: windmill at Blennerville

R559 signposted 'An Daingean'.
After passing a private church on the right, watch for **Kilmalkedar Church** on the left (90km/56mi ✝️⛪). Take a break to explore this roofless early Christian church set amidst old gravestones. Also of interest are the sundial on one of the gravestones and the ogham stones. If you walk up the track beside the graveyard and head left at a three-way fork, you can visit St Brendan's House, one of the finest stone-built romanesque houses surviving in Ireland.
A further 0.3km/0.2mi along the road there is yet another ruined church below on the right (✝️). Keep to the road for 0.3km/0.2mi more, and watch for a kissing gate on the right. This gives access to the very well preserved Celtic ring fort (⛪) shown above, built in a strategic position on a hillside overlooking Smerwick Harbour. From here continue along the main R559 straight back towards Dingle. Turn left at the T-junction in **Milltown**, cross the bridge, and turn right at the intersection just beyond it. Regaining the main roundabout in **Dingle** (98km/61mi), follow the signs to Connor Pass.
The views steadily improve as the road ascends between the Brandon and central Dingle mountains, but nothing quite prepares you for the spectacular outlook shown on page 111 — the panorama from the **Connor Pass★** (106km/66mi 📷). Looking north over the deep Owenmore Valley, studded with lakes in its upper reaches, you can see the beautiful bays of Brandon and Tralee with their long sandy beaches. At 952m/3123ft, Brandon Mountain is the second highest summit in Ireland. To the south there is a splendid view of Dingle Bay. Descending

from the pass, the road winds along the base of the precipitous Maughanablagher Cliffs. About 1.3km/0.8mi down the road, you curve through a corrie with a small waterfall tumbling down on the right (☂); it is fed by Lough Doon, just a little further up the glen.

Fork left for Brandon Point and turn left again at the following T-junction ('An Clochán'). Cross the Owenmore River and ignore the next left turn. Head through **Cloghane** (*An Clochán;* 114km/71mi ⌂🛏) and keep straight ahead at the next crossroads (where a right turn would take you to the fine sandy beach at Cappagh). Swing left and then right at the following junctions, to continue on the main road to **Brandon** (*Cé Bhréanainn;* 119km/74mi), another small coastal village with a post office and pier. Keep right on the main road beyond Brandon — to **Brandon Point** (121km/75mi ☎), where the road ends. Enjoy the marvellous view shown on page 4, across Brandon Bay to the mountains on the far side. Return the same way to recross the Owenmore. Now continue straight ahead past your original route on the right. The main road soon turns left and swings back right to cross a bridge. Very shortly, turn left across another bridge, ignoring a right turn just before it. Take the next left turn and cross a

stone bridge, to come to the car park at **Fermoyle Beach** (*Trá Fhormaoile;* 134km/83mi), a long sandy beach stretching for miles along Brandon Bay. Continuing the tour, soon rejoin the Tralee road and follow it straight on to **Stradbally** (⌂✕🛏). Turn left about 1.6km/1mi beyond the village on the road to the seaside resort of **Castlegregory** (160km/100mi ⌂✕🛏). Keep left at the first junction in the village and come to a crossroads. (Going straight ahead here, you could take a detour of 11km/7mi return along the sandy spit that separates the bays of Brandon and Tralee.) The main tour turns right on the R560 for Tralee. Following this main road out of Castlegregory, keep left at a junction, ignoring the right turn back to Stradbally.

Tralee Bay stretches out to the left, and there are several access roads down to the beaches. Near **Camp** the Slieve Mish Mountains are again close at hand. Stay ahead at a junction on the N86, with mountains to the right and the sea to the left. Before crossing the bridge at **Blennerville**, turn left to see the well-preserved windmill shown opposite (**M**). Then cross the bridge and follow the N86 — between the river Lee and a wide canal. Turn left at the roundabout into the centre of **Tralee** (*Traigh Li;* 'Beach of the river Lee'; 186km/116mi

Car tour 8: THE HAUNTING LANDSCAPES OF THE BURREN

Milltown Malbay • Lehinch • Liscannor • Cliffs of Moher • Lisdoonvarna • Black Head • Ballyvaghan • Aillwee Cave • (Kilfenora) • Corrofin • Dysert O'Dea • Ennis

107km/66mi; 3-4h driving

En route: Picnic (see *P* symbol and pages 8-11): 8; Walk: 14

All roads are in good condition.

This tour takes you through the varied landscapes in the Atlantic-facing northwest of County Clare. Beautiful bays fringed by sandy beaches alternate with steep rugged cliffs culminating in the famous Cliffs of Moher. Most intriguing is the strange lunar-like landscape of The Burren, a stark limestone region with caves, potholes, underground streams and other karst phenomena. The scarred rocky terrain is also famous for its rare flora, including many different kinds of orchids.

Leave **Milltown Malbay** (*Sráid na Cathrach;* ▲▲▲✕🍴) by heading north on the N67 towards Ennis. Turn left opposite the church in **Lehinch** (*An Leacht;* 'O'Connor's Cairn'; 12km/7.5mi ▲▲▲✕🍴), an attractive seaside resort at the head of Liscannor Bay. Turn left again at the next main junction, taking the R478 signposted to Liscannor and the Cliffs of Moher. Pass a golf course in the dunes and cross O'Brien's Bridge, to skirt round Liscannor Bay — fringed by some lovely sandy beaches. **Liscannor** (*Lios Ceannúir;* 17km/10mi ▲▲▲✕🍴▮) is a small fishing village popular with holiday-makers. Stay ahead on the main R478 to reach the car park at the famous **Cliffs of Moher★** (23km/14mi *i*📷*P*8; photograph overleaf). Continue on the R478 and keep straight ahead across the N67. Turn left at the next junction, cross the Gowlaun

River, and enter **Lisdoonvarna** (*Lios Dúin Bhearna;* 'Enclosure of the Gap-Fort'; 34km/21mi ▲▲▲✕🍴), a spa in pleasant surroundings, known for its iron- and sulphur-containing springs with their radioactive properties. Turn left in the town centre on the N67 to leave Lisdoonvarna. Then, at a junction where the N67 swings left, turn right and cross Murphy's Bridge. At a fork which comes up almost immediately, keep right on the R477. Now stay ahead on the R477, inoring a left turn below Ballynalackan Castle that rises up on a hillock to the right (▲▲▮).

Soon you're immersed in the strange and haunting landscapes of **The Burren★**, enjoying splendid views over its bare rocky limestone slopes. Pass a ruined church (♱) on the right at **Craggagh**, just a small scattering of houses, and keep left on the main road at the junction that follows

The Burren

Holy well near Black Head (top), pub at Craggagh, and coastal landscape. The countless holy wells in Ireland date back to ancient times, when water was a focus of Celtic spiritual life. Celtic Christianity later adapted this deep-rooted veneration of water. The well shown here is unusually elaborate, underlining the importance of this site. Other unusual features ramblers will stumble upon include ogham stones (page 34), round towers (page 79), ring forts and mass rocks. Ring forts (photo page 42) were the dominant domestic sites in the early medieval period and are still the most common monuments in the landscape. These circular farmsteads were defended by earthen or stone ramparts. Mass rocks were used as secret altars when Catholicism was still supressed. Out in the wilderness, a suitable rock would be chosen to serve as a makeshift altar.

almost immediately. Just 0.25km/0.15mi past a school on the right, you pass a left turn down to the car park at **Fanore Beach** (access to Walk 14). The road swings round to the right at **Black Head** (54km/33mi), where there is a lighthouse down on the coast to your left and far-reaching views over Galway Bay. Notice the holy well on the right by the roadside after another 5.3km/3.3mi (🍴; see above). Keep straight on past the church at **Ballyvaghan** (*Baile Uí Bheacháin;* 63km/39mi ⛽✕🍴), now following the N67 towards Lisdoonvarna. Take the left turn (R480) signposted to 'Corrofin, Ennis' not far beyond Ballyvaghan. Surrounded by smooth slopes, the road runs through a

The Cliffs of Moher, with O'Brien's Tower on the cliff-top (Picnic 8)

lush green basin opens up on the left, with ruined Carran Church (✝) standing by the roadside.

Continuing south past a couple of left turns, you come to **Leamaneh Castle** (⌂). Rising prominently on the right, the imposing ruins comprise a tall tower dating from 1480 and a 17th-century gabled house. Meet the R476 almost immediately. The main tour turns left here towards Ennis. (Turning right you could take a detour of 11km/7mi return to the Burren Display Centre (**M**) at Kilfenora.)

Pass straight through the villages of **Killinaboy** (✝●🅿) and **Corrofin** (🅿). Watch for a right turn about 3.2km/2mi beyond Corrofin, signposted 'church, round tower, cross, Dysert O'Dea'. Follow this road and keep right at the fork soon encountered. On coming to a car park not far from a ruined church (✝●), turn right across the cattle grid to a second car park at the castle, **Dysert O'Dea** (94km/ 59mi ◼).

To continue, return to the main R476 and turn right. Turn left when you meet the N85. Go straight ahead at a roundabout, following the signs into **Ennis** town centre (*Inis*; 'River-Meadow'; 107km/66mi *i*✝🏠🏠⛪🍴🅿⊕).

limestone basin. Watch for a sign on the left for Aillwee Cave and follow it, then keep right at the next junction.

Aillwee Cave ★ (67km/42mi 📷) is a limestone cave with fantastic dripstone formations. Back on the road, return to the main R480 and turn left. You wind uphill to a limestone plateau divided by beautifully-built drystone walls. A small sign alerts you to the **Gleninsheen Wegde Tomb** (🏮), a well-preserved dolmen to the left of the road — some 600m/yds on foot. Notice the many dolinas (karst depressions) all around. Another sign points the way to the **Poulnabrone Dolmen** (🏮), a further fine megalithic monument on the left. Soon a

Car tour 9: GALWAY, CONNEMARA AND JOYCE'S COUNTRY

Galway • Oughterard • Maum Cross • Recess • Roundstone • Clifden • Cleggan • Connemara National Park • Letterfrack • Kylemore Abbey • Leenaun • Cong

206km/129mi; 6-7h driving

En route: ♫ at Lough Mask; Picnic (see *P* symbol and pages 8-11): 9; Walks: 15, 16, 17

All roads are in good condition.

Connemara is a wild coastal region of outstanding natural beauty lying west of the vast expanse of Lough Corrib. The landscape is dominated by a high mountain range of conically-shaped hilltops known as the Twelve Pins — or, more traditionally, by their anglicised name: the Twelve Bens (from the Gaelic *Benna Beola*). Gaelic is still the local language in many parts of Connemara, which belongs to the western Gaeltachts. The ancient city of Galway, situated south of Lough Corrib where it empties into the sea, is the obvious gateway to Connemara.

Leave **Galway** (*Gaillimh;* 'Gailleamh's Place'; *i*♦🏨🏠✕🍴⊕) on the N59 to Clifden. Pass through **Moycullen** and **Rosscahill** before taking the signposted right turn to **Aughnanure Castle** (25km/15mi ◼), a medieval stronghold overlooking island-studded Lough Corrib. Resuming the journey, return to the N59 and turn right. Some 5km/3mi beyond **Oughterard** (*i*♦✕🍴), pass *The Quiet Man* bridge on the left, featured in John Ford's 1951 classic film. Continue ahead at **Maum Cross** (59km/37mi 🍴), following the scenic N59 through moorland, lakes and mountains. The road runs along the shores of several loughs, with the Maumturk Mountains looming on the right and the Twelve Pins (photograph page 119) rising majestically ahead. Beyond **Recess** (71km/44mi ♦🍴), the road skirts Glendollagh Lough, as the wide glaciated valley of

Glen Inagh opens up on the right, separating the Maumturks from the Twelve Pins. Pass the R344 on the right and the R340 on the left before turning left on the R341 towards Roundstone. Hidden in the woods to the right is Ballynahinch Castle (◼🏨), now an exclusive hotel. Soon after passing the entrance gate, an old station (now a private house) comes up on the right — one of the few remains of the old Galway to Clifden railway.

Pass the R342 to the left and go straight across the bridge. After 1.5km/0.9mi turn left on the main R341 into **Roundstone** (92km/57mi 🏨🏠✕🍴). Not far beyond this quiet little resort, short detours can be made to the lovely sandy beaches at Gorteen Bay and Dogs Bay. The road skirts Ballyconneely Bay and runs through the scattered houses of **Ballyconneely** (107km/67mi 🏠🍴) before skimming Mannin

47

*Left, top to bottom: Inishbofin
(Walk 17); Killary Harbour
(Walk 16); Ballynahinch Castle;
above: Connemara cottages*

Bay with its coral beach.
Take the signposted left turn to
the **Alcock and Brown
Monument** (112km/69mi
📷*P9*), for a glorious panoramic view over the coastal
region, with the Twelve Pins
rising further inland. This
memorial honours the achieve-
ment of John Alcock and
Arthur Whitten-Brown, the
first men to fly non-stop across
the Atlantic in 1919.
Return to the main road and
turn left to **Clifden** (*An
Clochán;* 'The Stepping-
Stones'; 117km/72mi *i* 🏨🏕✕
🚌), the main town of
Connemara and the centre of
Connemara pony-breeding.
Keep left to follow the one-
way system through the town.
Turn left at the next major
junction, following Sky Road.
Keep right at the next junction,
signposted 'Sky Road' again.

The road gradually winds up
the hill as you leave Clifden
behind. Bear left at another
junction to continue on Lower
Sky Road, with lovely views
over Clifden Bay. Go straight
ahead past any turnings. Upper
Sky Road rejoins from the
right shortly before the main
road swings inland and begins
to skirt Streamstown Bay.
Keep left at the junction at the
head of the bay and, when you
meet the N59 again, turn left.
Then leave the N59 after
2km/1.2mi (where it bends to
the right): continue straight
ahead to **Cleggan** (138km/
86mi 🏕✕🚌), a little fishing
village from where the ferry to
Inishbofin (Walk 17;
photograph below) departs.
Leave the village the way you
came in, but turn left for
Letterfrack after just
0.5km/0.3mi. The road skirts
Cleggan Bay before turning
inland to run above Ballynakill
Lough. Pass an old ruined
church on the right, peacefully
overlooking the lake (☎📷).

Turn right at the next junction, but keep left at the following Y-fork. The road skirts another lake before rejoining the N59. Turn left; Diamond Hill, one of the Twelve Pins, now rises straight ahead of you. You pass a car park on the left with a lovely view over Barnaderg Bay, before reaching the signposted right turn to the visitors' centre in the **Conne-mara National Park★** (151km/94mi *i*☎; Walk 15). On resuming the journey, proceed along the main road through the 19th-century Quaker village of **Letterfrack** (152km/94mi ♠✕🍽), little more than a crossroads sur-rounded by houses and pubs. The N59 skirts the foot of Diamond Hill, to enter the Pass of Kylemore. You pass the entrance to **Kylemore Abbey** on the left (156km/97mi 🏛✕), a 19th-century castellated mansion beautifully situated on the wooded shore of Pollacappul Lough. The house has been turned into a girls' school run by the Irish Benedictine sisters, but some rooms are open to the public. The N59 skirts Kylemore Lough before it passes the R344 forking off right through Glen Inagh. The Maumturks come into view on the right now, while Lough Fee appears on the left. Soon pass a left turn signposted 'Little Killary Adventure Centre, Killary Harbour Youth Hostel'. Continue for another 0.3km/0.2mi to the next turn on the left (where there is a small quarry just ahead on the right; 164km/102mi); this is where Walk 16 starts. The N59 crosses the Bunowen River before it begins to skirt the southern shore of Killary

Harbour. This spectacular arm of the sea (photograph opposite) runs inland between steep hillsides for about 16km/10mi; it is the only real fjord in Ireland (166km/103mi ☎).

The small village of **Leenaun** (*An Líonán;* 171km/106mi ♠✕🍽) nestles comfortably near the head of Killary Harbour. Leave the N59 here and turn right on the R336 for Maum. The road runs through an isolated valley amidst wild mountains. The whole area extending east to Lough Corrib and Lough Mask is known as Joyce's Country, named for the Joyces who settled here in medieval times. Watch for the signposted left turn to Lough Nafooey and follow this road over a gap in the hills, before beginning to descend to the lake. As you descend, follow the main road round a hairpin bend to the left (where another road continues straight ahead). Cross the Fooey River before skirting the northern shore of Lough Nafooey.

At the junction near the end of the lake keep right for Cong. Pass the church at Finny and cross an arm of Lough Mask on Ferry Bridge (🅿). Turn left at the junction in **Clonbur** (*An Fhairche;* 201km/125mi ♠✕🍽). Keep on the main R345 past any turnings until you reach **Cong** (*Conga;* 'Narrow Neck of Land [between two lakes]'; 206km/128mi ♠♠✕🍽). Stroll round this little village, with its ruined abbey (♦), riverside park with the monk's fishing house and curious dry canal. Ashford Castle (🅟❀🏰♠) is now a hotel, but its terraced gardens are worth a visit, too.

Car tour 10: MAYO, AROUND IRELAND'S SACRED MOUNTAIN

Leenaun • Aasleagh Falls • Delphi • Dhulough Pass • (Silver Strand) • Kilgeever Abbey • Murrisk and Croagh Patrick • Westport • Castlebar • Turlough Round Tower • Errew Abbey • Crossmolina • Ballina

127km/79mi; 4h driving

En route: Picnics (see *P* symbol and pages 8-11): 10a-b; Walk: 18

All roads are in good condition, but some lanes are narrow and winding.

County Mayo's varied landscapes range from sandy beaches and a rugged coastline to wild hills and sheer endless moorlands. But the most prominent feature is the holy mountain of Croagh Patrick, a conical peak rising 764 metres (2506 feet) above the shores of Clew Bay.

From **Leenaun** (*An Líonán* ⛰✕🍽), a small village near the head of Killary Harbour, follow the N59 north past a car park on the left overlooking the magnificent fjord (📷). Turn left at the very end of Killary Harbour on the R335 to Louisburgh. Soon cross the Erriff River on a bridge and leave your car at the car park on the left to take a look at the **Aasleagh Falls** (3.8km/ 2.4mi). Climb the stile on the far side of the road and follow the path along the beautiful river that tumbles down the hillside through the series of cascades shown below. The road skirts Killary Harbour (photograph page 48) before swinging north through the Bundorragha Valley, with Ben Gorm looming on the right. After crossing Delphi Bridge, you drive under a canopy of wild and romantic woods around Fin Lough. This beauty spot is called **Delphi** (13km/8mi), a name originally coined by Lord Sligo because of its similarity to the home of the Greek oracle.

Emerging from the trees, you enjoy a lovely view across Doo Lough, a long sheet of water trapped between the Mweelrea Mountains on the left and the Sheeffry Hills on the right. Follow the main R335 straight along the shore of the lake, a section known as the **Dhulough Pass** Road. Pass the left turn to Silver Strand at

Aasleagh Falls

Cregganbaun (22km/14mi) — or take it for an optional detour to some glorious sandy beaches along Mayo's west coast.

Continue on the main R335 for another 3.2km/2mi, before leaving it in a slight bend to the left, where you fork right on a minor road. Croagh Patrick rises prominently in the distance ahead. Ignore any turnings as you follow the road through rural countryside dotted with occasional houses. Stay ahead at the first crossroads, but turn right at the next one. Now watch for the second turn on the right, signposted to Kilgeever Abbey. This road takes you to a cemetery (32km/20mi), where you leave your car. Walk down the track that descends alongside the wall of the cemetery, to reach nearby **Kilgeever Abbey**, a ruined church set in an old graveyard (✝*P*10a). Note the holy well at the entrance gate.

Back in the car, return to the main road and turn right. Turn right again when you meet the R335 at **Kilsallagh** (34km/21mi). There are fine views across Clew Bay as you pass through the scattered houses of Leckanvy dotting the foothills of Croagh Patrick. Watch for the large car park on the right at **Murrisk** (*Muraisc*; 'Sea-marsh'; 41km/25mi); this is the starting point of the climb up Croagh Patrick (Walk 18; photographs pages 124-125). A small road on the left leads down to the nearby ruined 15th-century Murrisk Friary (✝), peacefully set on the seashore.

Carry on to **Westport** (50km/31mi *i*🏔🏠✕🚉⊕), a charming town originally laid out by the Georgian architect James Wyatt. The Mall is a pleasant avenue of lime trees

lining both sides of the channelled Carrowbeg River. Westport House, a fine Georgian mansion (🏛), is open to the public and well worth a visit. Follow the signs for the N60, to drive through Westport, cross the Carrowbeg River, and turn right immediately along the Mall; then turn left at the next bridge.

The N60 takes you straight into **Castlebar** (*Caislean an Bharraigh;* 'Barry's Castle'; 68km/42mi 🏨🛌✕🛒⊕). Follow the N5 out of town and through the small village of **Turlough**. Just 0.5km/0.3mi beyond it, turn left at a cross-roads (signposted 'Parke'). Then turn right at the next junction, to reach the well-preserved **Turlough Round Tower** (75km/47mi ⊙) on the right. Keep along this narrow road through the scattered houses of **Park** and turn right when you meet the main R310. Once in **Pontoon** (86km/54mi), a small village picturesquely sited between loughs Conn and Cullin, continue straight ahead at the junction.

Keep following the main R315 signposted 'Crossmolina/Lake Conn Drive'. Pass a car park on the right down on the shore of Lough Conn before going through the village of **Lahardaun** (97km/60mi 🛌✕🛒). When the R316 joins from the left, watch for the signposted right turn to Errew Abbey which comes up almost at once. Follow this narrow road, keeping left at a Y-fork, until it ends opposite a farm, in front of three iron gates (107km/67mi). From here it is only a short walk to **Errew Abbey**, peacefully set on a small peninsula projecting into Lough Conn (⚓*P*10b).

Return to the main road and turn right to pass Ennisco House/Maya North Heritage Center (*i*) on the right. Turn right at the first junction in **Crossmolina** (115km/72mi 🛌✕🛒) on the N59 to **Ballina** (*Béal an Atha;* 'Mouth of the Fjord'; 127km/79mi *i*🏨🛌✕🛒⊕). This, the largest town in Mayo, has a number of attractions, including a ruined friary (⚓) and the Dolmen of the Four Maols (⫪).

11 SLIGO, BENBULBIN AND YEATS'S COUNTRY

Sligo • (Rosses Point) • Rathcormack • Glencar Lough • Drumcliff • Cliffony • Mullaghmore • Gleniff Horseshoe • Manorhamilton • Dromahair • Lough Gill • Sligo • Carrowmore • Knocknarea • Strandhill • Sligo

149km/92mi; 5h driving

En route: Picnic (see *P* symbol and pages 8-11): 11; Walk: 19
All roads are in good condition.

County Sligo boasts some of the loveliest landscapes in Ireland, ranging from long sandy beaches to a mountainous hinterland with steep-sided and flat-topped limestone hills separated by wooded valleys. Most prominent are the Dartry Mountains, with the striking outlines of Benbulbin, Kings Mountain and Truskmore. This tour also takes in some of the places made famous in the poetry of Yeats, as well as his grave at Drumcliff. For those interested in archaeology, Carrowmore boasts the largest Stone Age cemetery in Ireland.

Start out in **Sligo** (*Sligeach*; 'The Shelly River'; *i* ♦ ♠♠ ♠ ✕ ⚏ ⊕), spread out in the wooded plain of the Garvoge River where it empties into Sligo Harbour. Head north along the main road, to reach a major road junction on the outskirts of Sligo. (Here you could turn left on the R291 for an optional detour of 15km/9.5mi to Rosses Point, a small seaside resort with a lovely sandy beach.) The main tour continues ahead on the N15. Leave the N15 at **Rathcormack** (5.6km/3.5mi ♠✕⚏) and turn right on a minor road past the church. Follow this road straight ahead, with Kings Mountain rising ahead of you. On coming to a T-junction, turn right. This road runs along the foothills of the Dartry Mountains which rise steeply on the left. Carry straight on past a right turn

and then, when you come to a T-junction, turn left. The road skirts beautiful **Glencar Lough**, affording fine views (☎) across the calm sheet of water to a mountainous backdrop overlooked by the rumpled heights of Castlegal. You come to a car park on the right (15km/9mi), opposite which a short footpath leads to Glencar Waterfall — immortalised by Yeats in his poem 'The Stolen Child'. Keep right at a Y-fork, meet the main N16, and turn right to continue. The old church of Glencar soon appears on the left (18km/11mi ♦). You come to a car park on the right, from where you enjoy the magnificent view (☎) shown opposite — over Glencar Lough with the impressive limestone escarpments of the Dartry Mountains rising precipitously beyond it. Follow the N16 for another

Left: Glencar Lake, with the Dartry Mountains in the background (Car tour 11)

Above: the ruined Franciscan friary of Killanummery, popularly called Creevelea Abbey (Picnic 11)
Left: Knocknarea. Be sure to carry a stone up to 'Maeve's Mound' at the top, to help make sure that the evil queen cannot escape...

4.5km/2.8mi, before passing a sign on the left: 'Caution. Dangerous bend ahead'. Fork right almost immediately beyond the sign on a minor road that takes you straight back to **Rathcormack** (29km/18mi). Here turn right on the N15, to reach the round tower and high cross at **Drumcliff** (30km/19mi ◉†), where Yeats's grave is in the churchyard.

Continuing on the N15, cross the Drumcliff Bridge and then take the first road on the left. Turn left at the junction in **Carney** and continue for another 2km/1.2mi, before taking the signposted left turn to **Lissadell House** (37km/23mi 🏛). From here return the same way to the junction in Carney, and now turn left, rejoining the N15 at **Cashelgarran**. The N15 runs north through a crossroads in

54

Mullaghnaneane (45km/28mi), where a right turn would take you to the start of Walk 19. You come into **Grange** (47km/29mi ♠✕🏪), set beneath flat-topped Benbulbin.

Go on to **Cliffony** (♠✕🏪), where you turn left at the crossroads on the R279; it runs along a promontory fringed by sandhills. Turn left again at a T-junction and keep right at the following Y-fork to reach **Mullaghmore** (51km/32mi ⛰♠✕🏪), a pleasant little resort and sailing centre with a lovely beach. The harbour was originally built by Lord Palmerston (1784-1865), who owned some land between Mullaghmore and Cliffony.

Follow the Cliff Drive in a counter-clockwise circle round the headland, past two left turns. There are far-reaching

Above: the Gleniff Horseshoe, a scenic road circling through a steep-sided glen cut into the flanks of the Dartry Mountains.
Right: Benbulbin (Walk 19) rises beyond Mullaghmore Harbour.

views across Donegal Bay and over to Classie Bawn Castle (■), once Lord Palmerston's mansion, before you rejoin your outward route. Head inland on the R279, but leave it where it forks right and stay ahead to meet the N15 at **Creevykeel** (57km/36mi ✕⛽). Your ongoing route will cross the N15 and continue straight ahead, but first turn left and watch for the car park on the right almost immediately, to visit the famous Creevykeel Court Tomb (П). Then return to the crossroads and turn left, following the sign 'Gleniff Horseshoe'.

Keep straight ahead at the next four crossroads, before beginning to follow the **Gleniff Horseshoe** road. It circles in a clockwise loop through the unspoilt Gleniff valley, a deep glen between the towering mountains of Truskmore (647m/2122ft) to the east, a summit that is easily recognisable by its radio mast, and Benwiskin (514m/1685ft) to the west. Turn right at a T-junction across the Ballaghnatrillick Bridge and, when you reach a crossroads almost immediately, turn left. Now follow your outward route back to the next crossroads and turn right. Pass through **Ballaghnatrillick** (74km/46mi) and carry straight on along the foothills of Tievebaun Mountain until you meet the main R280.

Turn right to continue through the fertile Bonet Valley, with eye-catching Glenade Lough as a centrepiece. **Manorhamilton** (*Cluanin Ui Ruairc;* 'O'Rourke's Little Field'; 96km/59mi ▲✕⛽) is sited at the confluence of four valleys. The town's major sight is the ruined baronial mansion built in 1638 by Sir Frederick Hamilton (⌂). Turn right at the main crossroads in the town centre, but take the next left turn, to meet the R280. Turn right again to follow this road out of town. It takes you southwest through the Bonet Valley past O'Donnell's Rock rising prominently on the left. Keep right on the R287 at the junction where the R280 turns left to Killarga, and stay ahead on the main road to **Dromahair** (*Droim Dhá Eithiar*; 'The Ridge of the Two Air-Demons'; 108km/67mi ⌂🛏✕🏠). Nowadays Dromahair is a tranquil village, but ruined Breffni Castle by the Old Hall (1626) was once a stronghold of the warlike O'Rourkes. In the village centre a signpost indicates a car park to the left, from where at pleasant footpath leads to Creevelea Abbey (🚶*P*11). Continue on the main R288 to leave Dromahair and skirt the northern shores of beautiful **Lough Gill**. **Parke's Castle** (116km/72mi ▮), on the left, is a restored 17th-century fortified manor house overlooking Lough Gill. The R286 soon begins to ascend into a region of low limestone hills and lush glens. Suddenly beautiful Colgagh Lough appears down on the right (121km/75mi 📷). Continue along the main road, and ignore a left turn signposted to Hazelwood Demesne (or take this optional detour, to a picnic area on the shore of Lough Gill).

When you meet a crossroads on the outskirts of **Sligo**, turn left into the town centre (127km/79mi). Go past the hospital, then turn left at a

major crossroads, to follow the one-way system. Cross a bridge over the Garvoge River and turn right into Castle Street at another crossroads. Now carry straight on past any turnings, through Grattan Street, John Street and Church Hill. Take the signposted left turn on the outskirts of Sligo to reach the car park at **Carrowmore Megalithic Cemetery★** (131km/82mi *i*🚻 📷), comprising the largest group of megalithic remains in the British Isles. There is free access to the numerous dolmens, stone circles, and cairns with sepulchral chambers scattered in the nearby fields. A local map is available at the visitors' centre.

Carry on to Redgate crossroads (🚶) and turn right. Keep left at a Y-fork, and turn left again at the following crossroads. Soon reach the signposted right turn to the Knocknarea Mountain car park (135km/84mi). This is where the short climb up **Knocknarea** (🚻; photograph page 54) begins. Malicious Queen Maeve of Connacht is said to be buried under a gigantic cairn called Miscaun Meadhbh ('Maeve's Mound') on the summit. Traditionally, each visitor carries a stone to the top to help build up the cairn, ensuring she never escapes.

Return to the main road and turn right to continue. Ignore any turnings until you meet the R292, then turn right, skirting the foothills of Knocknarea. Pass the seaside resort of **Strandhill** (141km/87mi 🛏✕) with its sandy beaches and follow the main road along Sligo Harbour back to **Sligo** (149km/92mi).

Car tour 12: ISOLATED LANDSCAPES IN THE FAR NORTH — DONEGAL

Donegal • Killybegs • Kilcar • Carrick • Bunglass •
Glencolumbkille • Glengesh Pass • Ardara • Dungloe •
Glenveagh National Park • Letterkenny • Barnesmore Gap •
Lough Eske • Donegal

371km/231mi; 12h driving

En route: ⌐ at Glencolumbkille, Lough Eske; Picnics (see *P*
symbol and pages 8-11): 12a-b; Walk: 20

All roads are in good condition.

Donegal, the most northerly county in Ireland,
offers varied landscapes ranging from the beautiful
indented coastline fringed by some lovely sandy
beaches to wild glaciated mountains and glens.
Glenveagh National Park, with its castle and gardens,
set around a lake in the wilderness of the Derryveagh
Mountains, is a further attraction. Donegal, at the head
of Donegal Bay, is a very pleasant town and an excellent
touring base where the main roads from Derry, west
Donegal and Sligo converge.

From the Diamond, the main
square in **Donegal** town (*Dun
na nGall;* 'The Fortress of the
Foreigners'; *i*🏛🏔🏔▲✕☎⊕),
head west along the N56
towards Killybegs. Pass
through the villages of
Mountcharles, **Inver** and
Dunkineely. Ignore the turn-
off (N56) to Ardara and stay
ahead on the main coast road,
now numbered R263.
Killybegs (*Na Cealla Beaga;*
'The Little Churches'; 27km/
17mi ▲✕☎) is one of Ireland's
foremost fishing ports. Make
sure you don't miss the arrival
of the fishing fleet when there
is bustling activity around the
pier.
Continuing on the R263, you
pass a couple of turns on the
left down to the nearby beach.
A viewpoint on the left
(33km/21mi ☞) takes in a
magnificent sweep of the coastline and Donegal Bay.
Continue for 1.6km/1mi, then
turn left on a minor road
signposted 'coast road'.

Beautiful seascapes unroll as
you follow this narrow lane
past Muckros Head. Turn left
at the crossroads in the quaint
village of **Kilcar** (*Cill
Charthaigh;* 41km/26mi
▲✕☎), the centre for Donegal
handwoven tweeds, and
continue along the coast road.
A fine outlook over Teelin Bay
opens up on your left as you
wind through the rural
countryside.
Turn left at a T-junction and
follow this road towards
Carrick. Turn left across the
bridge into **Carrick** (*An
Charrig;* 47km/29mi ▲✕☎)
and keep left at the Y-fork just
beyond it. Then take the first
turn on the left (at the post
office), to make for the cliffs of
Bunglass and Slieve League.
Keep left at a Y-fork, following
signposting for 'Bunglas/The
Cliffs' (ignore the sign 'Slieve
League' ahead).
Once through the hamlet of
Teelin (*Teileann;* 50km/31mi
▲), take the signposted right

turn by the school ('Bunglass/ The Cliffs'). Climb this road as it winds up the hill past occasional houses. Not far beyond the last house, go through an iron gate and continue climbing past Lough Meeraviller and Lough O'Muilligan, both on the right, to reach the car park at the end of the road (54km/33mi 🎦). The magnificent cliff scenery at this viewpoint, **Amharc Mór**★ ('The Great View'), is absolutely breathtaking. Far below, breakers crash constantly against the **Cliffs of Bunglass** which rise sheer out of the water to a height of more than 300m/1000 feet (see photograph page 129). Slieve League, the highest peak along this coast, is explored on Walk 20.

Return the way you came through Teelin, heading towards Carrick, but take the first turn on the left almost immediately after crossing Carrick Bridge at the end of Teelin Bay. Soon meet the main R263 and turn left. Ignore the left turn to Malin Beg and continue straight ahead. Some 4km/2.5 miles past this junction, a detour on the left leads to a good viewpoint over the peaceful Glencolumbkille valley, dotted with whitewashed houses (67km/42mi 🎦🚏P12a). Continue descending the road into the valley, to reach **Glencolumbkille** (*Gleann Cholm Cille;* 'St Colmcille's Glen'; 69km/43mi ♠✕🚏M), a quiet village rich in ancient monuments.

Stay ahead on the main road, ignoring the R263 to the left, and go past the post office. On

meeting a T-junction, turn right for 'Ardara, Glengesh' and follow this road across a bridge over the Murlin River. Keep right at the Y-fork immediately beyond this bridge, driving through a gap in the hills. You meet another road in the hamlet of **Meenaneary** (*Mín an Aoire;* 77km/48mi 🚏); turn left here. Stay ahead as this road gradually climbs through the valley of the river Crow. At **Glengesh Pass** a viewpoint on the left affords a spectacular outlook down over the steep-sided valley of Glengesh (87km/54mi 🎦). From here the road plunges down into the valley to meet the main N56 at the bottom.

Turn left for **Ardara** (*Ard an Rátha;* 'The Rath Heights'; 94km/58mi ♠✕🚏). Cross the Owentocker River in the town centre and continue ahead on the R261 at the junction soon

afterwards. Heading north, the road passes through a wild landscape studded with lakes. Keep left at a Y-fork near a church (signposted to the twin holiday villages of Narin and Portnoo overlooking Gweebarra Bay). Leave the main R261 where it bends right and continue ahead on a minor road to **Irishtown** and **Narin** (also spelled Naran; *An Fhearthainn;* 204km/127mi ♠). Leave your car at the car park and take a pleasant stroll along the lovely sandy beach. At low tide, Inishkeel Island can easily be reached on foot. Now return the same way, but keep left when you reach a Y-fork at the end of the village. Keep left again at the next junction and follow the R261 through **Clooney**. On meeting the N56, turn left and head north through an isolated coastal region studded with lakes. **Dungloe** (*Clochán Liath;*

229km/143mi *i*♠♠♠✕🖵⊕) is the main town in this remote corner of Ireland known as The Rosses (*Na Rosa;* 'The Headlands'). Turn right on meeting the main through road. Stay ahead on the R259 until you reach a road junction some 1km/0.6mi short of Burtonport. The airport is signposted to the right, but keep left to visit **Burtonport** (*Ailt an Chórrain;* 237km/147mi ♠✕🖵), an important fishing village from where the ferry sails to Aran(more) Island. Return the same way you entered the village, but keep left at the road junction, this time following the airport sign. The road skirts Keadue Strand on the left and runs along a causeway. Keep left at the junction just beyond it, following the sign for Anagaire. The road winds through secluded villages and

59

Corn and flax mills at Newmills

past a left turn to Donegal airport before it meets the N56. Turn left and follow this road past any turns, until you can turn right for Glenveagh National Park (signposted). This well-built road (R251) affords splendid views down into the valley on your right, where Lough Nacung can be seen, followed by Dunlewy Lake further east. To the left rises Errigal, the highest mountain in County Donegal. Ignore a right turn down to Dunlewy at the eastern end of the lake. You pass a couple of viewpoints on the right (268km/167mi ☎), from where the glaciated Derryveagh Mountains can be seen in the southeast. The steep-sided corrie opening in the mountains bears the forbidding name Poisoned Glen.

The road gradually veers northeast to traverse a vast boggy plain fringed by high mountains, before leading down to **Glenveagh National Park** (283km/176mi *i*🏛 ✕*P*12b). You have to leave your car in the designated parking area near the visitors' centre, where you can pick up some information leaflets. There is a regular minibus service between here and Glenveagh Castle which is surrounded by pleasant formal and informal gardens (❀). After visiting the park,

continue along the main road before taking the first right turn to Church Hill. Watch for a sign on the right to Saint Colmcille's Birthplace and Abbey and take this country lane. Another sign on the right points up to Saint Colmcille's Abbey (⚓), a small ruined church with a cairn topped by a stone cross and a nearby holy well. Continue to another right turn signposted to Saint Colmcille's birthplace. This short drive takes you to a car park at a road junction, from where you continue on foot along the field track to the left. It leads to the reputed birthplace of the saint, marked by an ancient flagstone and a more recent Celtic cross (🏛⚓). Continue across Tehabber Bridge to **Glebe House and Gallery** (295km/183mi 🏛❀), beautifully set in woodland gardens on the shore of Gartan Lough. Soon rejoin the R251 and turn right. Beyond **Church Hill** (*Mín an Labáin*; 297km/185mi ☕), the road affords beautiful views over the surrounding countryside. Stay ahead on the main road past any turnings. Watch for a sign on the right pointing to the **corn and flax mills at Newmills** as the road begins to follow the river Swilly (307km/191mi **M**). You can step back in time with a visit to these old mills which are still in action, operated by a large water wheel.

The main road continues through the Swilly Valley to **Letterkenny** (*Leitir Ceanainn*; 'The Hillside of the O'Cannons'; 314km/195mi *i*🏛🏠✕☕⊕**M**). Turn right at

Glenveagh National Park (Picnic 12b)

the first roundabout and left at the second one. At a third roundabout (where a left turn would take you into the town centre) turn right, following the sign 'N14/Sligo'. At the next roundabout take the third exit, the N56 south. This takes you through a partly-wooded landscape, to a T-junction where you turn right for Donegal. When you meet the N15 in **Stranorlar** (*Srath an Urláir*; 334km/207mi ♠ ✕ 🏠), turn right to pass through the twin village of **Ballybofey** (*Bealach Feich*). The N15 continues along wooded hills before passing through **Barnesmore Gap**, a wild glaciated glen flanked by steep heath-covered mountain slopes — once a haunt of

much-feared highwaymen and robbers.

As the valley begins to open up, take the signposted right turn to Lough Eske. Stay ahead on this small country lane until you reach a junction. Turn right to begin your scenic drive round **Lough Eske**. You enjoy beautiful views over the peaceful lake on your left, set amidst green fields and woods, with the Blue Stack Mountains rising in the distance. Ignoring any turnings, you come to a good viewpoint (361km/ 224mi 🚏🎥) and then carry on to a crossroads, where you turn right for Donegal. When you meet the N56, turn left back into **Donegal** (371km/231mi).

Car tour 13: THE ANTRIM COAST AND THE GIANT'S CAUSEWAY

Glenarm • Carnlough • Cushendall • Cushendun • Murlough Bay • Ballycastle • Carrick-a-Rede • Giant's Causeway • Bushmills • Portrush

115km/71mi; 4h driving

En route: ⋔ in the Glenariff Forest Park; Picnics (see **P** symbol and pages 8-11): 13a-c; Walks: 21, 22

All roads are in good condition. The corniche north of Cushendun is extremely narrow, with steep gradients and sharp bends; drive carefully.

From towering cliffs to white sandy beaches and from tranquil glens to lush forest parks, the Antrim coast unfolds its unique beauty as you make your way north, close to the water's edge. This scenic route takes you past some of Ireland's most beautiful seascapes, with a superb succession of vistas at almost every turn. Steeped in legend, the Giant's Causeway is famous for its polygonal rock formations — nearly 40,000 columns of dark basalt jutting out into the sea. Not for the faint-hearted is the famous Carrick-a-Rede rope bridge, spanning a 20m/60ft chasm between the mainland and an offshore islet.

Start out in the pretty village of **Glenarm** (⌂✕⌂▪), situated in a small bay at the mouth of the eponymous glen, one of the famous nine glens of Antrim. Follow the coast road (A2) north to **Carnlough** (3.3km/2mi ⌂✕⌂) at the mouth of Glencoy. Its houses are spread around a lovely bay fringed by a sandy beach, while the harbour is popular with the yachting crowd.

Continue round the steep escarpments of Knockore, forming the headland of Garron Point, to reach the next bay at **Glenariff** (also known as **Waterfoot**). Here the most famous of the Antrim glens, Glenariff, stretches inland between steep hillsides — the lower slopes covered by a patchwork of fields, the upper reaches densely wooded. The glen is now a lovely forest park with waymarked footpaths and pleasant picnic spots. Turn left at the T-junction in Glenariff to head inland on the A43. A

Dunluce Castle

signposted left turn leads to the car park in the **Glenariff Forest Park** (28km/17mi; Walk 22; ⌂*P*13a).

Return to the main A43 and turn left to continue. Soon turn sharp right for Cushendall (B14). Descend past a left turn down to **Cushendall** (42km/26mi *i*♠✕♟), a pleasant town near the northern end of Red Bay. Notice the old tower (■) in the centre: it was originally built as a lock-up for 'idlers and rioters'. Rejoin the main coast road (A2) and turn left to follow it out of town.

Watch for the signposted right turn to Cushendun and take it. **Cushendun** (50km/31mi ♠) is a quaint village with white-washed houses located at the southern end of a sand-fringed bay. Fork right not far beyond the village on a minor road signposted to Torr Head and Ballycastle. This narrow corniche winds its way north along steep hillsides, affording superb views of the coastline and across the North Channel to Scotland. Keep left at a junction for Ballycastle and ignore two more right turns, both signposted to Torr Head. Follow the road through mountain bog, before taking the signposted right turn to beautiful **Murlough Bay★**. This road leads to an unspoilt bay of great scenic grandeur with lush vegetation covering the sheltering cliffs. The road runs uphill at first, then winds its way down to the coast past several car parks. Leave your car on the right-hand side of the road a short way before the asphalt peters out near the water's edge (where a sign warns 'road liable to subsidence'; 68km/42mi). For a short leg-stretcher, follow the track ahead past an old kiln and a lonely house on the right to an unspoilt sandy beach (*P*13b).

Return the same way you came

Left: Carrick-a-Rede rope bridge; above: Antrim coast near Glenariff Forest Park (Walk 22)

to the main road and turn right to continue. When you meet a T-junction, turn right for Ballycastle. You pass a right turn to Fair Head before rejoining the main A2 in **Ballyvoy**. Turn right to reach the seaside and port of **Ballycastle** (79km/49mi *i*⌂▲✕🚏⊕). Now follow the signs for the Giant's Causeway through Ballycastle, to leave the town on the B15. Heading west, you reach a right turn to the car park near the famous **Carrick-a-Rede★** rope bridge shown above (88km/55mi). A short cliff-top path, affording magnificent views to the west coast of Scotland, takes you to the famous bridge which spans a wide chasm between the mainland and Carrick-a-Rede island. It is put up in April each year by local salmon fishermen who use the bridge to get to the fishery on the island.

Continue on the B15 through **Ballintoy** (▲). Not far beyond the village there is a car park on the right offering an excellent view of the coast (📷). Ignore a signpost on the

right to White Park Bay but, not far beyond this junction, fork right on the B146, signposted to the Giant's Causeway. After less than a mile the insignificant ruins of **Dunseverick Castle** appear on a rock to the right (96km/60mi ⬁); this is where Walk 21 ends. Continue along the B146 to reach the car park and visitors' centre at the **Giant's Causeway★** (101km/63mi *iMP*13c; Walk 21).

From here continue on the B146 to meet the A2 and turn right to **Bushmills** (104km/65mi ⌂✕🚏), where you can visit the oldest licensed distillery in the world. At the roundabout in the town centre, turn right (signposted to Portrush), to stay on the A2. Ignore the turn-off for Portballintrae, but watch for a signposted right turn to the impressive ruin shown below — **Dunluce Castle** (108km/67mi ⬁), perched on a rock overlooking the coast. Continue on the A2 towards Portrush. You pass a car park on the right from where there is a good view along the coast with its fine sandy beach (📷). Ignoring the turning right to White Rocks Beach, the main tour heads straight into **Portrush** (115km/71mi *i*⌂▲✕🚏⊕), one of the leading seaside resorts in Northern Ireland.

14 COUNTY DOWN — A LIVING HERITAGE

Newtownards • Mount Stewart • Portaferry • Strangford • Castle Ward • Downpatrick • Ardglass • Newcastle • Silent Valley • Spelga Dam • Tollymore Forest Park • Castlewellan • Downpatrick • Comber • Newtownards

212km/131mi; 7h driving

En route: ⍚ at Strangford Lough, Crocknafeola Wood, White Rock; Picnics (see *P* symbol and pages 8-11): 14a-b

All roads are in good condition. See ferry details on p134.

More so than any other county in Ireland, Down is remarkable for its green rolling hills, with a patchwork of walled fields covering the rich and fertile soil. In striking contrast are the Mourne Mountains, an upthrust of granite through the older Silurian rock. Beautiful Strangford Lough, the largest sea inlet in the country, is separated from the sea by the Ards Peninsula. Fine resorts and quaint fishing villages line the beautiful coastline that boasts some excellent sandy beaches. Among the many ancient monuments and historic sites in County Down is the reputed burial place of Saint Patrick, the patron saint of Ireland, close to Downpatrick Cathedral.

From **Newtownards** (*i*♠✗➿⊕) head southeast on the A20 along the Ards Peninsula, following the signs for Portaferry. Soon the vast expanse of Strangford Lough comes into view on the right (⍚ at 6.7km/4.2mi). The road skirts the eastern shore of this large island-studded sea inlet and passes an extensive estate, **Mount Stewart** (8.8km/5.5mi 🏛❀), with a beautiful house and gardens.

Turn left at the roundabout in **Greyabbey** and right at the next T-junction. There is a car park on the right almost at once in front of the ruined Cistercian abbey which has given the village its name (13km/8mi ✝). Return to the roundabout and continue on the A20. Head south along the peninsula to **Portaferry** (32km/20mi *i*♠♠✗➿ M), a strategically-sited town over-looking the narrows connecting Strangford Lough with the sea.

Take the car ferry from here to **Strangford** (♠♠✗), a quaint village with a picturesque harbour. It was named by the Vikings who encountered powerful currents rushing through the narrow strait; in Old Norse it means 'strong fjord'. Follow the A25 towards Downpatrick, but turn right at a signposted crossroads to **Castle Ward** (36km/22mi 🏛❀), a mansion of unusual architecture set in beautifully-landscaped grounds.

Return to the crossroads and turn right to continue. Watch for a sharp right turn signposted to Audley's Castle. This short foray takes you to a well-preserved and strategically-situated towerhouse guarding the 'strong fjord'. Follow the small

65

country lane before turning left on the signposted gravel track. This leads past some huge oak trees to the foot of a mound with **Audley's Castle** perched on top (43km/27mi ▮).

On resuming the journey, return to the main road and turn right. (An optional detour to the Quoile Countryside Centre (**M**) can be made by taking a sharp right turn shortly before reaching Downpatrick. There is a ruined castle beside this nature reserve which comprises a large expanse of freshwater wetland.) The main tour continues on the A25 to a T-junction, where you turn left. Reach a roundabout almost immediately and take the first exit to enter the county town of **Downpatrick** (55km/34mi *i*✝ ▲▲✕☎⊕**M**) where fine examples of Georgian and Victorian architecture can be found. Saint Patrick is reputedly buried in the churchyard★ adjacent to the cathedral at the western edge of the town.

Follow the signs for Ardglass through Downpatrick. Watch for an unexpected turn on the left, to join the B1, and turn right soon afterwards to stay on this road. Notice a left turn at the edge of town, signposted to the Struell Wells, and take it for a short visit to this tranquil place. Stay ahead on the small country lane until a sign diverts you to the right. The **Struell Wells** buildings (59km/37mi ✝⚏⌂P14a) comprise a ruined church, drinking well, eye well (holy water) and bathhouses in a lovely setting.

Return to the main B1 and turn left to the charming fishing village and former royal port of **Ardglass** (70km/43mi ▲✕☎▮). Turn right at the junction on the A2, to **Killough** (74km/46mi), a quaint old village with just one row of houses around a small bay. Go straight through the village and follow the road ahead to St John's Point. After turning left at a junction, St John's Point Church (✝) comes up on the left. The west door, built before the introduction of the arch, testifies to its great age. Continue to the lighthouse at **St John's Point** (78km/48mi). Then go back to the last junction and turn left. The road soon begins to skirt Dundrum Bay, fringed by some long sandy beaches. Rejoin the main A2 and turn left to continue. Pass a turning left to Tyrella Beach and continue on the main road to **Clough** (94km/59mi ☎▮). At the T-junction in the village, turn left to reach **Dundrum** (98km/61mi ▲✕☎▮). Stay ahead on the A2, past Murlough Nature Reserve on the left, an area of extensive sand dunes with a National Trust information centre. Soon you reach **Newcastle** (104km/65mi *i*▲▲✕☎⊕), a popular seaside resort at the western end of Dundrum Bay. Go straight through Newcastle and head south along the coast road, with the sea to the left and the Mourne Mountains looming to the right. Some 10.5km/6.5mi beyond Newcastle, take a right turn signposted 'Silent Valley via Scenic Route'. This road (C313) climbs inland towards craggy Slieve Binian, affording magnificent views over the patchwork of walled fields, with the Mournes towering in the background. Follow the

Nendrum: these remains of a 5th-century monastery are one of the best examples of an early Christian monastic enclosure in Ireland.

road round a sharp bend to the left, now skirting the hillside. Stay ahead on this road until it swings left. Fork right on this bend, through the gate, for a visit to the **Silent Valley** (112km/70mi *i*WC). Return to the main road and turn right to continue, then fork sharp right almost immediately, following a sign to Spelga Dam. Ignore minor turns on both sides, but turn right when you meet the main B27. Again you enjoy magnificent vistas as you head into the mountains. You pass Crocknafeola Wood on the left (⊼ at 118km/74mi). The road ascends a glaciated valley with steep slopes on either side rising to Pigeon Rock Mountain on the left and Slieve Muck on the right.

When Spelga Dam comes into view on the left, you can safely stop at one of the lay-bys and enjoy the view. Stay ahead on the C312 at a Y-fork and follow the sign for Bryansford, ignoring the left turn to Hilltown. The road leads over a gap in the hills before descending through the Shimna Valley. Pass another

artificial lake on the right known as Fofanny Dam. When you meet the B180, turn right to **Bryansford** (132km/82mi). Turn right at the end of the village (signposted 'Tollymore Forest Park') and turn right again through the Barbican Gate. A fine avenue leads into **Tollymore Forest Park** (135km/84mi ✕*MP*14b). When you leave through the exit gate, turn right to pass through Bryansford again. Go past the right turn you took earlier, and stay ahead on the B180 until you meet the A50. Turn left and follow this road into **Castlewellan** (140km/87mi ▲✕▆). Turn right in the town centre, following the signs for Downpatrick. Take the signposted left turn opposite Castlewellan Library for a visit to Castlewellan Forest Park, featuring an excellent arboretum, an aviary, elegant Queen Anne-style farm courtyards and several waymarked trails around a lake.

Continue on the A25 through **Downpatrick** town centre (161km/100mi) and keep straight ahead at the

Country code for walkers and motorists

The experienced rambler is used to following a 'country code' on his walks, but the tourist out for a lark may unwittingly cause damage, harm animals, and even endanger his own life. A code of behaviour is especially important in Ireland, where you often cross private land, and where the boggy and desolate terrain can lead to dangerous mistakes.

Photograph: Rhododendron ponticum

- **Do not frighten animals.** The sheep and cows you may encounter on your walks are not tame. By making loud noises or trying to touch or photograph them, you may cause them to run in fear and be hurt. Grazing land is rarely fenced off: in spring, motorists should be extra vigilant. Young lambs tend to follow the mother ewe closely. If you see a young

roundabout on the outskirts. Ignore a right turn to Castle Ward almost immediately; keep ahead on the A22. (There is a turn on the right to Delamont Country Park after 168km/104mi, a detour not included in the mileage.) Pass through **Killyleagh** (🛏🔺✕🏛), birthplace of the naturalist Sir Hans Sloane, whose extensive collections formed the nucleus of the British Museum, and stay on the A22 to reach **Balloo** (179km/111mi 🏛).

At the entrance to Balloo fork right to **Cillinchy** and descend the road to Strangford Lough. Turn left along the shore; White Rock, beside Sketric Island, is a modern yachting centre (⛺🏛 at 183km/114mi). When you meet a T-junction, turn right for Comber. On coming to another T-junction almost at once, turn right again, to pass through the village of **Artmillan**.
Follow the main road through rural countryside. Ignore all

- lamb on one side of the road and an adult on the other side, be prepared to stop; the young lamb may run across the road to its mother.

- **Stay on the path** wherever it exists, to minimise damage to surrounding vegetation. Don't take short-cuts on zigzag paths; this hastens ground erosion.

- **Leave all gates just as you found them**, whether they are at farms or on the mountainside. Although you may not see any animals, the gates have a purpose: they are used to keep sheep or cows in (or out of) an area.

- **Protect wildlife, plants and trees.** Don't try to pick wild flowers or uproot saplings. Obviously fruit and other crops are someone's private property and should not be touched.

- **Dogs** should never be taken on any of these walks, as they distress livestock and wildlife.

- **Take all your litter away with you.**

- **Do not damage fences and stone walls**; use gates and stiles where they exist.

- **DO NOT TAKE RISKS!** This is the most important point of all. Do *not* attempt walks beyond your capacity, and do not wander off the paths described if there is any sign of mist or if it is late in the day. **Do not walk alone**, and *always* tell a responsible person *exactly* where you are going and what time you plan to return. If you park your car at the beginning of a walk, you can leave a note on the seat. Remember, if you become lost or injure yourself, it may be a long time before you are found. On any but a very short walk near villages, be sure to take a first-aid kit, whistle, torch, extra water and warm clothing — as well as some high-energy food, like nuts and chocolate.

---

turnings until you meet a T-junction, then go right. But leave this road almost immediately when it bends left: continue straight ahead on a minor road. This takes you along two causeways via Reagh Island onto Mahee Island in Strangford Lough, where you can visit 5th-century **Nendrum** (194km/121mi 🚻). Return the same way to the main road and turn right to continue. You pass a turn on the right to Castle Espie at 201km/125mi; this nature reserve, run by the Wildfowl and Wetlands Trust, is ideal for observing water-birds. On meeting the main A22, turn right into **Comber** (205km/127mi ⬧✕☎). At the junction in the town centre, turn right on the A21 towards Newtownards. Note Scrabo Hill on the left, an impressive formation of red sandstone and basalt that is now a country park. Follow the main road straight back into **New-townards** (212km/131mi).

✾ Walking

In recent years walking in Ireland has become very popular. Increasingly, both locals and visitors alike are beginning to explore the varied countryside on foot. Those willing to put up with unstable weather and boggy ground will be rewarded with unexpected and spectacular walking opportunities. This book covers some of the best walking in Ireland, with a slight emphasis on the wild mountainous west of the island. For a quick orientation, the fold-out touring map shows the general location of all the walks.

The book has been designed to introduce you to walking in Ireland as *safely* as possible. *Do* follow the notes closely and don't try to cross boggy ground (which might prove dangerous) or private land (where you might not have right of way) unless I explicitly advise you to do so.

There are walks in the book for everyone.

Beginners: Start on the walks graded 'easy', and be sure to look at the short and alternative walks as well — some are easy versions of the long walks.

Experienced walkers: If you are used to rough terrain and have a head for heights, you should be able to tackle all the walks in the book, *provided that conditions are still as described in the notes*. Of course, you must take into account the season and weather conditions. For example, in rainy weather some river crossings will be impassable; in strong winds or mist do not plan excursions to the mountains. Always remember that **storm damage or flooding can make some of the routes described in this book unsafe**. Remember, too: always follow the route as described in this book. If you have not reached one of the landmarks after a reasonable time, you must go back to the last 'sure' point and start again.

Waymarking, guides

Most of the walks in this book use clearly-defined footpaths, trails and tracks that are all easily followed (although there is also the odd bit of cross-country walking). **Waymarking** of walks is minimal, and there is very little signposting, so you will have to rely entirely upon the descriptions and maps in this book.

Some of my walks incorporate short sections of officially waymarked routes — like the Wicklow Way, the Beara Way or the Burren Way. These ways were set up throughout Ireland in the 1980s and 90s and now comprise over 2000 kilometres (1200 miles). Owing to the lack of trails, they involve a lot of cross-country bog walking as well as some tiresome stretches along asphalt roads. The development and maintenance of these ways is coordinated by the National Sports Council (COSPOIR), with the cooperation of the Bord Fáilte (the Irish Tourist Board), COILLTE (the Forest Board), local authorities, private landowners and devoted local voluntary workers. All these routes are waymarked at frequent intervals with standard COSPOIR signposts. These are usually black wooden posts with yellow arrows indicating the route; sometimes they also show the symbol of a walker. On difficult sections the posts tend to be quite close together; on easy sections, with little chance of getting lost, they may be more widely spaced. Where such waymarking is significant along the route of my walks, I refer to it.

Excellent **guides** are available in Ireland, mainly in the Wicklows and in the west of the Republic, but none is needed for the walks in this book. Guided tours are organised regularly by walking clubs and specialist tour operators. Anyone wishing to explore the more remote and wild mountainous regions not described in this book is well advised to do so in the company of a local guide.

Maps

The maps in this book have been adapted from the 1:50,000 Discovery Series. These excellent Ordnance Survey maps cover the whole of Ireland in 89 sheets. They were originally published as a result of collaboration between the two surveys. The sheets covering the Republic are called the Discovery Series and published by the Ordnance Survey of Ireland, a government department, while those covering Northern Ireland are called the Discoverer Series and published by the Ordnance Survey of Northern Ireland.

The maps for my walks have been specially annotated to tie in with the text with, for instance, the addition of specific landmarks. They should be sufficient for all the walks you plan using this guide. Nevertheless, if you wish to purchase the original sheets or additional ones, they are readily available at petrol stations, in bookshops and at local tourist offices. You can also order them directly from your local map stockist.

Right of way

Much of Ireland's land is in private hands. There are no statutory, but many recognised rights of way. The walks in this book follow these routes as far as possible or have been given the blessing of the land-owner. Generally speaking, most landowners, whether tenant or farmer, are reasonable as long as you respect their property.

There is, however, always an exception to the rule. In a few cases, landowners or tenants have tried to dis-courage walkers by posting 'private' signs. This does not usually affect the mountain walks (nobody bothers there), but land around farms. Should you encounter any difficulty, tell the owner politely where you wish to go. Please *do* respect him and leave his property if he asks you to do so. And please inform Sunflower Books, so this information can be passed on to other walkers in 'Updates'.

What to take

If you are already in Ireland when you find this book, and you haven't any special equipment such as a rucksack or walking boots, you can still do some of the walks — or buy yourself some equipment at one of the sports shops. *Don't* attempt any walk without the proper gear or with brand new footwear. For each walk in the book the *minimum year-round equipment* is listed. Where walking boots are required, there is no substitute: you will need to rely on the grip and ankle support they provide, as well as their waterproof qualities. All other walks can also be made with stout lace-up shoes.

You may find the checklist on the next page useful. Please bear in mind that I have not done *every* walk in the book under *all* conditions. For this reason I have listed under 'Equipment' all the gear you *might* need, depending on the season, and I rely on your good judgement to modify the list accordingly.

walking boots (which *must* be
  broken-in and comfortable)
waterproof rain gear (preferably
  'Goretex' or similar)
fleece jacket
long-sleeved shirt
long trousers
cardigan
woollen hat and gloves
spare bootlaces
compact folding umbrella
rucksack
extra pair of socks
telescopic walking stick(s)
plastic bottle with water
  purifying tablets
first-aid kit, including bandages,
  plasters and antiseptic cream
plastic plates, cups, etc
knives and openers
plastic groundsheet
sunglasses, sunhat, sun cream
insect repellent
compass, whistle, torch, mobile

Climate and weather

Ireland's climate is characterised by prevailing westerly winds, abundant precipitation and moderate temperatures throughout the year (hardly dropping below freezing at sea level). This maritime climate is considered 'mild' in terms of the vegetation it supports, but such a term is relative, of course… and 5°C/40°F on a windy day in pouring rain certainly don't *feel* mild if you are out in the hills! So it is important to choose the right time of the year to get the most out of your walking holiday.

Ireland is a green island — for good reason. There are in fact some 200 wet days annually in the north and west. But it rarely rains *continuously* for more than a few hours each day, since the weather tends to be quite changeable. According to a popular Irish saying, you can have all four seasons in a single day — at least during the winter months. As a general rule, there is about twice as much rainfall in the mountains and on the coast than further inland. If clouds engulf the hilltops, and dense mist prevents you from going into the mountains, you could still consider a low-level walk — along the coast, for example.

The climate or general weather pattern should be borne in mind when planning a holiday in Ireland. During December and January depressions bring strong winds and heavy rain. Snow is rarely seen on the coast, but higher ground will have occasional snowfalls from November to April. From February to June the cold European highs tend to produce the driest period of the year. February often has the advantage of clear skies and frosty air, but the days are still short and, unless the temperature is below freezing, the ground tends to be even wetter and more boggy than during the rest of the year.

In spring, dry cold spells guarantee crisp days with brilliant sunshine — excellent for hill-walking. From late spring until early summer the terrain is much drier than during the rest of the year, and the lush vegetation, with a profusion of wildflowers, is at its best. May typically sees an average of 6-7 hours of bright sunshine per day and is the ideal month for walking.

Towards late June damp westerly winds begin to flow over Ireland, producing more clouds and increasing precipitation for the rest of the summer. In autumn, fresh westerlies bring more rain. They are occasionally interrupted by brief anti-cyclonic conditions producing clear sunny days.

Another Irish saying has it that when you see the hills it's going to rain, and when you cannot see them it's already raining. But the weather certainly isn't all that bad if you choose the right time of the year. You will enjoy many a day in Ireland that is hot and sunny — so sunny in fact that you may get sunburnt. You have of course to reckon with the odd rainy day, and waterproofs are an essential part of the walker's equipment, but in summer adequate sun protection is just as important, especially up in the mountains and by the sea.

Mountain safety
The following points cannot be stressed too often:

- **At any time a walk may become unsafe due to storm damage, flooding or erosion**. If the route is not as described in this book, and your way ahead is not secure, do not attempt to go on.

- **Walks for experts only** may be unsuitable in winter, or very wet after heavy rain. *All mountain walks may be hazardous after heavy rain.*

- **Never walk alone**; four is the best walking group. If someone is injured, two can go for help, and there will be no need for panic in an emergency.

- **Do not overestimate your energies.** Bear in mind that most accidents happen on the descent, when you are tired, so take extra care. Your speed will be determined by the slowest walker in your group.

- **Plan your walk carefully**, and be sure you can complete it before dark; estimate your total walking time generously including breaks (see page 77).

- **Transport** connections are vital.

- **Proper walking shoes or boots** are a necessity.

- **Mist and rain** can suddenly close in, not only on the higher elevations. *Do* check the local weather forecast and don't be deceived by *brilliant* sunshine in the morning — a very bright morning is almost invariably followed by thick clouds gathering later in the day.

- **Warm clothing** is needed in the mountains; even in summer take some along, in case you are delayed. Normally the temperature drops almost 1°C for each 100m/300ft of ascent.
- **First-aid kit, compass, whistle, torch** weigh little, but might safe your life. The mountain distress signal is six blasts per minute and then a pause.
- **Extra rations and plenty to drink** must be taken on long walks, including high-energy food like nuts and chocolate.
- **Take a sunhat and adequate sun protection** with you in summer.
- A **telescopic walking stick** is a great help on rough or steep terrain.
- **In case of emergency**, telephone 999 or 112 and ask for the Mountain Rescue or contact the local *garda* (in the Republic) or police station.
- Read and re-read the important note on page 2, the country code on pages 68-69, and the guidelines on grade and equipment for each walk you plan to take.

Where to stay

Ireland offers a wide range of accommodation in all categories and prices. Most places are listed in the official guides which are published annually. Published by Bord Fáilte, the *Accommodation Guide* covers the Republic, while *Where to stay in Northern Ireland* is issued by the Northern Ireland Tourist Board. Gradings and prices for the places listed in these guides are compulsory. Advance booking is advisable in the busy summer months of July and August. Bookings for registered premises can be made direct by phone or through tourist offices (for a small charge). From October to Easter, many of the smaller establishments close, so it is a good idea to check with the tourist board which houses will still provide accommodation.

Bed and breakfast accommodation is very popular with tourists, especially in the Republic. Many houses (easily recognized by their signs) provide B&B. Some are officially approved; others are not registered. The standards vary somewhat, but most establishments are very welcoming and clean, with en suite bathrooms. The full Irish breakfast served at the B&Bs is, of course, one of their great attractions — cereal, followed by bacon, egg, sausage and tomato, along with whole-grain soda bread, toast and marmalade. B&Bs usually don't need to be booked in advance, but in season it is advisable to check in by midday or early afternoon at the very latest to avoid the 'evening rush' for vacancies.

Hotels are far more expensive, but sometimes they offer special weekend rates. They usually have bars where meals are provided. Hotels are mainly found in the cities and tourist resorts and are rare in the more secluded areas.

Hostels are quite popular with young people and all types of outdoor enthusiasts. There are official hostels — An Óige in the Republic, YHANI in Northern Ireland — as well as a large number of privately-owned places classed as Independent Holiday Hostels (IHH); other establishments fall under no particular umbrella. Hostels have become an attractive alternative to B&Bs — they are much cheaper and a far cry from the spartan facilities of traditional hostels. Moreover, you have kitchen facilities at hand and can cook your own evening meals. Dormitory accommodation is still predominant, although an increasing number of hostels offer family rooms. Both An Óige and YHANI hostels require membership of Hostelling International (HI). They are closed during the daytime and have evening curfews (… officially anyway). Independent hostels can vary greatly, depending on the owner but, generally speaking, the atmosphere is more relaxed and sociable. Also, there are no curfews and you don't have to be out during the daytime. In the summer it is advisable to book your hostels in advance.

For those wishing to spend an entire week at the same place, quaint **Irish cottages** are also available for rent. Most of these cottages cluster in small, newly-built tourist villages, so inquire in advance if you are after solitude.

There are also many sites for **camping** and **caravanning**. In view of the lack of facilities, unstable weather, boggy terrain and privately-owned land, rough camping is *not* recommended.

Organisation of the walks

There are 22 main walks in this book, spread across the most scenic regions in Ireland. I hope that the book is set out so that you can plan your walks easily — depending on how far you want to go, your abilities and equipment, and the season. Wherever you are based in the popular tourist areas, there should be a walk within relatively easy reach. However, most of the suggested walks are *not* accessible by public transport.

You might begin by looking at the large fold-out touring map at the back of the book. Here you can see at a glance the overall terrain, the road network, and the location of the walks. Quickly flipping through the book, you'll see that there is at least one photograph for every walk, to give you an idea of the landscape.

Having selected one or two potential excursions from the map and the photographs, turn to the relevant walk. At the top of the page you'll find planning information: distance/time, grade, equipment and how to get there. *Pay particular attention to the ascent —* more than 500m/1600ft is pretty tough going for the average walker. If the grade and equipment specifications are beyond your scope, don't despair! There is sometimes a short or alternative version of a walk, and in most cases these are far less demanding of agility and equipment.

When you are on your walk, you will find that the text begins with an introduction to the overall landscape and then quickly turns to a detailed description of the route itself. The large-scale maps (see notes on page 71) have been annotated to show key landmarks. **Times** are given for reaching certain points in the walk, based on an average walking rate of 4km per hour and allowing an extra 15 minutes for each 100m/330ft of ascent. These time checks are *not* intended to predetermine *your* pace! They are meant to be useful reference points, so *do* compare your own times with those in the book on a short walk, before you set off on a long hike. Only brief pauses are included — where you might stop to catch your breath or orientate yourself. Perhaps increase the times by one third, to allow ample time for protracted breaks — picnicking, photography and nature-watching.

Below is a key to the **symbols** on the walking maps:

▬▬▬	main road	●►	spring, fountain, etc	♱	church or chapel
▬▬	secondary road	*P*	picnic suggestion (see pages 8-11)	†	oratory or shrine
▬	minor road			○	ring fort
▬	unsealed road, lane	☜	best views	⊠	post office
-----	track, wide trail, etc	🚌	bus stop	*i*	visitors' centre
·········	footpath (or no path)	🚗	car parking	🛋	picnic tables
—400—	height (metres)	⚓	ferry	🏛	transmitter.pylon
2→	main walk	■	building	📖	map continuation
2→	alternative walk	■ ◻	castle, fort.ruins	⛏	ancient site
		⚒ ∩	quarry, mine.cave	⚡	power station

Walk 1: GLENDALOUGH — THE MONASTERY, THE SPINK AND POULANASS WATERFALL

See map pages 82-83; see also photos pages 16-17, 18, 83
Distance: 15.6km/9.8mi; 5h20min
Grade: strenuous, with ascents of 580m/1900ft overall. Not recommended when there is poor visibility and a chance of low cloud.
Equipment: walking boots, wind/waterproof jacket, walking stick, picnic, water
How to get there and return: 🚌 St Kevin's bus from Dublin to/from Glendalough's visitors' centre or 🚗 to/from the first (lower) car park at Glendalough (the 122km/76mi-point on Car tour 1).

Shorter walks
1 Lower circuit along the slopes of Derrybawn Mountain (7.5km/4.7mi; 2h20min). Easy. Total ascent of 170m/560ft. Access and equipment as above, but no walking boots required. Follow the main walk to the wide junction of tracks (1h40min) and take the first track downhill to the right. Now follow the main walk from the 4h35min-point back to the car park.

2 Upper circuit across The Spink (9.4km/5.8mi; 3h25min). Moderate. Total ascent of 480m/1575ft. Access: 🚗 or 🚌 to the second car park at the Upper Lake (the 124km/77mi-point in Car tour 1 and **P**1c). Equipment as above. From the car park, follow the footpath to the Upper Lake. Turn left on meeting a tarmac track close to the shore of the lake and follow it over a wooden bridge, crossing a small river. Leave the track on the first bend to the right, to climb the footpath ahead beside Poulanass Waterfall. A short ascent on steps flanked by wooden railings takes you along the mountain brook that tumbles down the wooded ravine on the left and through a series of gorgeous cascades and pools. After a short while you emerge on the forest track again and follow it further uphill. Turn sharp right at a wide junction of tracks (15min), then follow the main walk from the 1h40min-point to the 4h35min-point.

*G*leann dá Loch, the 'valley of the two lakes', is one of the most important early Christian sites in Ireland. The monastery was founded by Saint Kevin during the 6th century and existed for a millennium before it was finally demolished under Cromwell. Most buildings, including St Kevin's Church, an ancient barrel-vaulted stone oratory, are clustered near the Lower Lake. Glendalough exudes an aura of peace and tranquillity that must have attracted Saint Kevin some 1400 years ago. Take your time to absorb the spiritual atmosphere of this valley, where architecture and landscape combine in such a magical way. This delightful walk climbs above the monastery, with tantalising views out over the whole valley and, on a clear day, across the entire Wicklow range.

Round tower at Glendalough. Round towers developed under the threat of Viking raids in the early Christian period. They served as lookout posts and defense towers for the monasteries.

Set out from the car park at **Glendalough** by turning left in front of the visitors' centre and cross the wooden footbridge over the **Glenealo River**. Meet a 'green road' almost immediately (**3min**) and turn left. Flanked by moss-covered stone walls, this old grassy trail takes you under a canopy of foliage, through mixed woodland — oak, beech and holly. Note a wooden signpost on your left; it marks a short detour you should take … down to **St Saviour's Priory** (**18min**), a ruined church in the lush green river flats of the **Glendasan**. Rejoin the green road and turn left to continue. Before long branch off sharply to the right and pass a barrier, to climb a forest track. It gradually ascends the hill, swinging left at first and then back right again. Ignore a fork to the left and stay ahead, to reach another junction where you also keep straight on. This track now contours the hill for the next 20 minutes, affording pleasant views to the right over the woody Glendalough Valley.

At the next junction, keep right and begin to descend. Cross two wooden bridges further down in the valley and reach a wide JUNCTION OF TRACKS almost immediately (**1h40min**). Ignore the fork down to the right: take the next track, which is almost opposite. *(But Shorter walk 1 descends to the right here, and Shorter walk 2 joins here.)*

Follow the track uphill for a short way, but leave it on the first bend to the left and take the path on the right way-marked with a red arrow. This boardwalk path leads all the way uphill through the conifers. As the ascent levels out, cross a stile and continue along the boardwalk.

You have now reached **The Spink** (**2h07min**), and it becomes clear that this buttress is just the projecting nose of the long Lugduff ridge that flanks the southern side of the Vale of Glendalough. Looking back, you get superb glimpses of the Lower Lake with the monastery just behind it. The famous round tower stands out clearly against the other buildings.

The boardwalk runs straight across the ridge. *A word of caution:* Stay on the boardwalk and don't venture to the right, since there is a sheer drop into the valley. Eventually the boardwalk path begins to climb in earnest, soon reaching a vantage point affording a magnificent view of the old

79

miners' village at the head of the valley (see Walk 2).

The path continues beside an old rotten fence, with a plantation of adult conifers to the left. Soon you begin to lose sight of the valley. Your route briefly runs along a boardwalk once more, before widening into an old trail that gradually ascends straight along the left-hand side of the heather-covered ridge. *(Walk 2 joins via a boardwalk coming in from the right.)*

Your trail is cut into a thick layer of turf which can occasionally be seen. Climbing more steeply, it finally swings to the left (by a waymarking post with a red arrow), now following the contour of the hill, with spectacular views on the left over partly-reafforrested hillsides. Sometimes stony, sometimes grassy, your trail is always clearly visible: it runs just a few metres/yards above the line of some old wooden posts.

You leave the rotten fence behind when you reach a waymarker post with a red arrow painted on it. Your trail veers slightly left at this point and begins to descend the hillside to a wide flat SADDLE (**3h35min**). Here again a welcoming boardwalk leads you over boggy ground. The bare rounded hilltop of **Mullacor** (657m/2155ft) rises ahead. Once down in the middle of the saddle, turn left at the boardwalk T-junction (where you meet the **Wicklow Way**). Within 30m/yds you reach the tree line, where you will pick up a forest track. Descend this track to the left through conifers, following a short section of the Wicklow Way. Keep left at the wide junction encountered about six minutes later and continue downhill along this bulldozed track. Turn sharp left after another four minutes, leaving the Wicklow Way and descending through a partly waterlogged clearing between the conifers.

The rest of the walk is quite straightforward. Bear left at a junction and follow the forest track below **Prizen Rock**, round the head of the valley. It gradually begins to descend along the far side of the valley below the southern flanks of The Spink. Ignore a sharp right turn after about 20 minutes and keep straight on.

Vale of Glendalough, with the Upper and Lower lakes

Pass the path you climbed on your outward route and veer right around the hairpin bend, to regain the wide TRACK JUNCTION (**4h35min**). *(Shorter walk 1 rejoins here, and Shorter walk 2 returns to the car park.)*

Turn sharp left on the downhill track, but leave it soon, descending a footpath on the right signposted to the **Poulanass Waterfall**. Flanked by wooden railings, this very pleasant descent takes you by a wooded gully on the right with a mountain brook tumbling noisily down through a series of cascades and pools. The pale green colour of the water is caused by the suspension of tiny flakes of mica. Poulanass means 'the hole of the waterfall' and probably refers to one of the larger plunge pools. Holly and oak trees provide pleasant shade as you descend.

Emerge on the track again and continue straight downhill across a wooden bridge. You will turn right on the signposted green road immediately after crossing the river but, before doing so, wander over to the nearby shore of the **Upper Lake**, to take in the sheer beauty and positive energy of this setting (**4h50min**; *P*1c). The alleged site of **Saint Kevin's Cell** is on a rocky spur up the wooded cliff to the left.

Now continue along the green road that begins at the wooden bridge and follow this pleasant old trail past the **Lower Lake**. A signposted left turn takes you across a wooden footbridge to the CHURCHES AND ROUND TOWER (**5h15min**). Leave the monastic site through the main entrance and turn right immediately, to go past a gravel-strewn car park. Cross a wooden footbridge over the **Glendasan River** to regain the visitors' centre at **Glendalough** (**5h20min**).

Walk 2: GLENDALOUGH — ALONG THE UPPER LAKE INTO THE GLENEALO VALLEY

See photographs pages 16-17, 18, 75, 79, 80-81
Distance: 8km/5mi; 3h30min
Grade: moderate, with a steep climb of 220m/720ft up the valley beyond the old miners' village, and another climb up to The Spink. The walk is (sparingly) waymarked throughout with white arrows.
Equipment: walking boots, water, picnic
How to get there and return: 🚌 St Kevin's bus from Dublin to/from the Upper Lake at Glendalough or 🚐 to/from the second car park at Glendalough (the 124km/77mi-point on Car tour 1).

Short walk: The old miners' village (4km/2.5mi; 1h return). Easy; no ascent. Access and equipment as above, but no walking boots or picnic required. Follow the notes below to the old miners' village and back.

Fringed by wooded cliffs, the Upper Lake is peace-fully set in the Vale of Glendalough. The magical beauty of this landscape is further enhanced by its sense of wilderness and isolation. This walk takes you along the north side of the Upper Lake to a deserted mining village, from where you can venture further up the Glenealo Valley — at its best in the morning, before the tourists flood in, and when the sun shines in from the east. If you're lucky you will spot deer, kestrels and other birds of prey.

Start out from the car park at **Glendalough** by following the tarred footpath to the Upper Lake. Turn right on meeting a tarmac track close to the shore and follow it across a wooden bridge that takes you over the **Glenealo River**. Just beyond it, turn left on the old **Miners' Road** and walk along this road. The asphalt soon ends below an Education Centre;

continue straight ahead on the gravel track. It leads you along the wooded northern shore of the **Upper Lake**, hemmed by tall, thick-trunked Scots pines. These trees were planted in 1856/57 by the mining company for use as pitprops but, fortunately, mining in the Glendalough area ceased before these trees were cut.

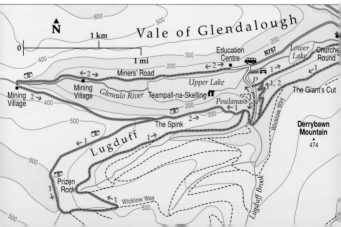

On the opposite shore, about 10m/30ft above the surface of the lake, you can spot a small cave known as Saint Kevin's Bed — where the saint is said to have spent his days and nights in contemplation. Further to the right are the 6th-century ruins of Teampall-na-Skelling, or 'the church of the rock'. These comprise the oldest monastic buildings in the Glendalough area. The only access is by boat.

Continue west towards the head of the valley, with the swampy bed of the Glenealo on your left, to reach the old MINING VILLAGE (**30min**), where the track ends. Spoil heaps of waste rock and some ruined buildings testify to buzzing mining activity during the 19th century. The miners' village was then a principal mining centre in the Wicklows, with a mill for crushing the rock containing galena (lead ore). The tailings reservoir can still be seen today; it is the square-shaped pond just west of the Upper Lake.

Now venture further up the valley. From the mining village, follow the north bank of the river round a meander, to cross some large boulders strewn along the valley floor. Join the old, once stone-cobbled miners' track that twists steeply uphill beside the Glenealo. Looking back, you enjoy spectacular views over the valley and lake below. You approach the spoil heap of a derelict MINE on the left; the old track leading to it can be seen on the far bank of the river. But the old bridge across the Glenealo is long gone, so your trail keeps climbing through rocks along the right-hand (northern) side of the river, crossing some tributaries on small log bridges. Eventually a wooden footbridge leads you across the Glenealo to the far bank where you pass some RUINS belonging to the mine (**1h25min**).

Continue ahead on the way-marked path, soon following a boardwalk over boggy terrain. Gradually rising above the Glenealo Valley, you eventually join a path running on top of **Lugduff ridge**: continue straight ahead in an easterly direction. You are now following a section of Walk 1 in the reverse direction. Soon you reach a spectacular VIEW-POINT (**2h30min**) out over the whole valley.

Keep following the boardwalk straight ahead along the ridge. Beware of leaving the route — there is a sheer drop on the left down into the valley. Cross a STILE (**3h**) near the end of the ridge and descend the fairly steep boardwalk into the conifers. When you meet a forestry track, turn left down-hill, to reach a wide TRACK JUNCTION (**3h15min**). This is the 4h35min-point of Walk 1. Turn sharp left and follow the notes on page 81 past **Poulanass Waterfall** and down to the car park at **Glendalough** (**3h30min**), where you started out.

Walk 3 LOUGH DAN

Distance: 6.7km/4.2mi; 2h15min

Grade: easy, but halfway along you have to cross the Cloghoge River on slippery stepping stones, wade through it, *or retrace your steps.* Total ascent of 220m/720ft.

Equipment: sturdy shoes, water, optional picnic

How to get there and return: 🚌 to/from the 64km/40mi- point on Car tour 1, where the second private road turns off left from the Sally Gap road through a gate in a stone wall. There is a sign prohibiting all motor cars, but walkers are allowed to enter. Leave your car by the side of the main road, but don't block either of the turn-offs. There is also another car park a little further along the main road.

Hidden in the heart of the Wicklows, a secluded mountain lake awaits your discovery. Along this walk you will also come upon a number of derelict farmsteads tucked away in the beautiful Cloghoge Valley. They are the puzzling remnants of an old settlement abandoned during the Great Famine. Except for a somewhat tricky river crossing, the route is very straightforward and easy to follow. This is a 'classic' walk to be savoured, so take your time and enjoy the beautiful setting, with peaceful Lough Dan embedded in it like a gemstone.

Start out by the **Sally Gap road**: walk through the gate flanked by two stone pillars. The black iron gate is usually open but, if it is closed, just use the adjacent pedestrian gate. Descend the small tarmac lane, looking down into the impres-

sive glen through which the Cloghoge River flows from Lough Tay to Lough Dan. A patchwork of long-abandoned fields with extensive traces of past cultivation can be seen opposite, on the slopes of Luggala or 'Fancy Mountain'. Fork sharply left downhill (still on tarmac) by a cottage that was once the KEEPER'S HOUSE AND POST OFFICE (**13min**), ignoring the entrance gate to the grounds of Luggala Lodge; there is a sign 'Lough Dan 2 Irish miles' on the wall. (So far the Irish have not let me in on their secret of what an *Irish* mile really is. Probably they're not entirely sure, either.) Some grand Scots pines and oaks grace the slope down on the right as you descend further into this peaceful glen.

Pass another beautiful pair of old stone pillars and note the right-hand pillar: the curious steps built inside it once served as a stile. Carry straight on along the field track at the three-way junction, where there is a farmstead on the left. At the bottom of the valley, a wooden bridge takes you over the **Cloghoge River**. Soon you cross another small bridge across the **Cloghoge Brook**, a tributary of the main river: it flows down the side valley separating Luggala from Knocknacloghoge. Carry straight on at the fork immediately beyond this bridge along the grassy old trail or 'green road', crossing the stile by the middle iron gate.

Your trail is flanked by a neatly built stone wall on the left. As soon as the woodland on the left ends, peer over the wall to get a first glimpse of some RUINED BUILDINGS dating back to the Great Famine. You can reach this abandonded homestead, a little community consisting of at least three houses, by turning left through a gap in the wall; the gate is usually open (**33min**).

Continuing along the green road, pass another ruined dwelling on the right, where you can still see the old fireplace. There is a typical *haggard* (kitchen garden) behind this house, enclosed by a stone wall.

The valley floor down on your left is covered with lush pastures where sheep graze peacefully. You will see some strange circular stone constructions in the fields; their original purpose seems to have been forgotten, but it *is* known that there were still trees growing in the middle of them a few decades ago. I think they were originally meant to be shady seats. If you have a better idea please let me know!

Old farmhouse at Lough Dan

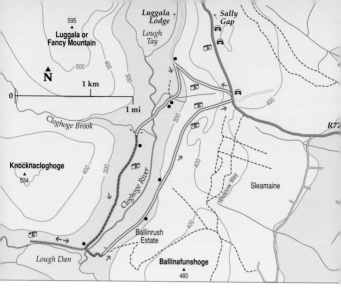

Pass through two iron gates that must be kept closed and reach a lonely two-storey farmhouse dwarfed by a grand beech; before you is **Lough Dan** (**1h**). At the turning point of the walk, this place makes a perfect picnic spot, and, if you come here on a weekday, you may have it all to yourself. The shutters of this lovely farmhouse are always closed, and the door is always locked. You can sit and relax in front of the house or on the sandy beach where the Cloghoge River flows into the lake. You could also venture further along the trail; it narrows to a path and runs above the northern shore through gorse before petering out at the end of the lake — another scenic resting spot, where you could sit on the rocks up on the right.

For your ongoing route you have to cross the Cloghoge River just east of the cottage on stepping stones that can be quite slippery in wet weather... so have your camera ready! Alternatively, you could wade through the river, but it can be quite deep after rainfall. Once you have negotiated this somewhat tricky river crossing, the rest of the walk is quite straightforward. Follow the path uphill through mixed woodland and past an old farmstead on the right. When you reach the main gate of the **Ballinrush Estate** (**1h10min**), turn left uphill on the track. Then just carry straight on, ignoring all side turnings for the rest of the walk. You pass a cottage up on the right and a roofless house on the left soon after, with four large beeches sprouting up from the middle of the ruins. Pass another house on the right and go through a white iron gate. A green iron hut on the left, with some bizarre paintings on its walls, will leave you shaking your head in bewilderment. Enjoy lovely views out over the Cloghoge Valley and your outward route, with Lough Tay coming into sight in the north. You pass through a green iron gate and emerge on the **Sally Gap road** just where you've parked your car (**2h15min**).

Walk 4: ALLIHIES AND THE SLIEVE MISKISH MOUNTAINS

Distance: 16.5km/10.3mi; 5h40min

Grade: moderate, with ascents of 620m/2030ft overall on well-defined tracks or lanes. Except for a very short section, this circular walk follows the Beara Way, marked by black posts with a yellow walker and an arrow indicating the way in both directions.

Equipment: walking boots, wind/waterproof, water, picnic

How to get there and return: 🚌 to/from Allihies — on the R575 near the western end of the Beara Peninsula, reached via Eyeries or Castletown-Bearhaven (the 72km/45mi-point on Car tour 5).

Copper Mine Museum: open Mon-Fri 10.00-17.00 (closed 13.00-14.00 Thu/Fri); Sat/Sun 12.00-17.00

On this pleasant ramble you wind your way round the hills of the Slieve Miskish Mountains. Allihies is a quiet village off the beaten track, situated on the foothills near the western end of the Beara Peninsula. The scarred hillsides above the village testify to copper mining that started in the early 1800s but has long since ceased. These are the mines where Daphne du Maurier's novel *Hungry Hill* is set. The walk also unveils green fields, woodland and stunning vistas over the surrounding seascapes.

Start out in **Allihies** by heading south along the main road (the **Beara Way**), passing the church on the left, soon followed by the post office. Ignore a sharp turn on your left and continue straight ahead past the **Copper Mine Museum** on your left, housed in the old Methodist church. Turn left at a road junction by the last house, following a lovely *bohereen* running between old drystone walls (there is a signpost here for the Beara Way). This intimate field track, fortunately not yet tarmacked, twists its way down through fields and crosses a small concrete bridge over the **Ballydonegan River** (**10min**). Gradually you begin to emerge from the valley. You will see the old mine shafts on your left, overlooked by a deserted engine house rising some

distance away, but *do* heed the warning signs and don't venture into the fenced-off areas. When you meet a small asphalt road, turn left, ignoring a right turn almost immediately. Go past another road that turns off to the right at an acute angle, and reach the few houses of **Kealoge** (**35min**). Turn sharp right here, up the small asphalt road, and follow it round a bend to the left, going uphill through a farmstead. Continue up the road, past a driveway on the left. This easy ascent affords magnificent views across the Caminches Valley to the Slieve Miskish Mountains rising beyond it. Spread out on the bare limestone slopes are the old copper mines, with a couple of engine-houses clearly silhouetted. Leave the asphalt road where it

bends left towards the summit of Knockgour and follow the track ahead (notice a couple of standing stones in the bog on your right just before reaching this junction). Your track skirts a conifer plantation beside wooden electricity poles. Soon leave the trees behind; there is a sweeping view on your right over turf-laden hillsides.

At the top of the rise, where the track is cut deeply into the turf, you cross over a SADDLE between Knockgour looming on the left and an unnamed ridge on the right (**1h55min**). Superb vistas of the southern flanks of the **Slieve Miskish Mountains** begin to unravel, with Bear Island rising beyond the narrow strait of Bear Haven.

Reach a junction almost immediately and continue ahead, following signs of the Beara Way. Walk down the track, pass a left turn, and go over a crossing track. Soon continue ahead on a gravel road that joins from the right. On reaching the bend of a small asphalt road, turn left along it. You pass through the mostly deserted hamlet of **Knockoura**; just two houses are still inhabited (**2h20min**).

Just beyond some ruined houses on the left, turn sharp left up a gravel road. Fork right at a junction, to continue on a grassy track along the tree line, with lovely views of the waters around Bear Haven and Bear Island. Cross a stile and follow the grassy track as it swings left uphill through conifers. Then look for the driest path you can find through a waterlogged

Ruined engine house

gravel track where the tarmac lane turns off right. A steady climb takes you along the northern flanks of **Knockoura**, with fine views over the scattered houses of Urhin dotting the slope down on the right. Across the Kenmare River bay, the distant hills of the Iveragh Peninsula can be seen. At the top of the rise you cross a GAP IN THE RIDGE, cut into slanted limestone strata (**5h05min**). Suddenly there are magnificent views over Allihies down on the fertile coastal plain.

The gravel road gradually winds down through the DISUSED COPPER MINES. The curious ruins, spoil heaps and reservoirs on the scarred hillside bear strange witness to the past. *A word of caution:* Stick to the road and don't venture into the fenced-off areas of the old mineshafts, where the ground is liable to subsidence. The prominent ruin of an ENGINE HOUSE (see above) comes into view on the left, as the gravel road acquires a tarmac surface. Leave the road on a left-hand bend below the engine house (now up on your left) and follow the signposted Beara Way down to the right. The path descends past some foundations on the left, to an electricity pole with a transformer. Continue ahead on the gradually-widening path. It is stony at first, then becomes grassy and waterlogged. Cross a stile and pass some ruined houses. Go through a wooden gate, descend the trail to a small asphalt road and turn right. Meet the main road immediately and turn left back into **Allihies** (**5h40min**).

section in a small clearing. Emerging from the trees, your track turns right downhill along an old wire-mesh fence. Pass through more conifers, cross a stile, and then meet the BEND OF A TRACK (**3h**). Leave the Beara Way here and turn left downhill.

Dominated by Knockoura on the left and Miskish Mountain on the right, the track zigzags down through the **Travara Valley**. The descent offers sweeping views over the open hillsides, with the blue waters of Coulagh Bay shimmering beyond the coastal plain. Pass an iron gate by some sheep pens and keep left at the Y-fork soon after. You have now rejoined the **Beara Way**. Turn left on meeting a small asphalt road in the hamlet of **Aughabrack** (**3h35min**). Follow the road ahead past the odd house, but leave it some 50m/yds after it bends to the right and turn left up a minor tarmac road.

Keep straight ahead along the

Walk 5: BEAR ISLAND

See photograph page 34
Distance: 13km/8.1mi; 4h15min
Grade: easy climb of 380m/ 1245ft with moderate ups and downs, but route-finding demands some sense of orientation (the posts numbered 9-27 mostly indicate a direction rather than a path). The moorland section of the

walk can be waterlogged after rain. No shade.
Equipment: walking boots, wind/waterproof jacket, water, picnic, sunhat; compass an advantage
How to get there and return: 🚐 no 282 or 🚗 (the 34km/ 21mi-point in Car tour 5) to/ from Castletown-Bearhaven, then ⛴ to Bear Island.

Bear Island — *An tOileán Mór* ('the big island') in Gaelic — lies well off the beaten track. The west of the island is sparsely populated, with just the occasional house abutting the main road. Three Martello towers and a signal tower testify to the island's strategic position in days gone by. In the more recent past Bear Haven served as an important 'treaty' port for the British Navy, where Dreadnought battleships were moored until as late as 1938. This circular moorland walk takes you to the lighthouse at the western tip of the island and on to the signal tower. You enjoy a striking panorama from the highest rise on the island, before returning along the main road.

Getting to **Bear Island** on the old ferry (more rust than iron as some terrified passengers invariably tend to note) is an experience in itself. Once you're back on *terra firma*, **head off** from the PIER along the road leading uphill. Turn right at a road junction, following a sign for 'The Beara Way/Bear Island' (**14min**). Turn left at the end of the main track (**22min**), cross a stile by the iron gate and follow the track uphill. You'll notice a number of old blockhouses on the hillside to the right. Keep on the track and cross a couple of stiles by iron gates; there is a house nearby.
Leave the track soon, veering slightly left up a path ascending the partly-rocky hillside; a white arrow painted on a rock confirms your route. Posts nos

1-8 follow in quick succession. Soon the route descends and passes a fenced-in blockhouse on the right, before climbing some stone steps uphill. When you meet an old grassy lane at POST NO 8 (**47min**), turn left along it, ascending gradually. It bends left and then right, before leading to the light-house at **Ardnakinna Point** (**1h02min**).
Turn left uphill above the lighthouse, following POST NO 9. The next part of the walk leads cross-country through boggy ground, generally in a easterly to northeasterly direction. At POST NO 13 you meet an old trail with stabilized stony banks (**1h25min**): turn right along it, but leave it soon (at POST NO 14) where you fork left. The next few posts lead straight up the hill in an

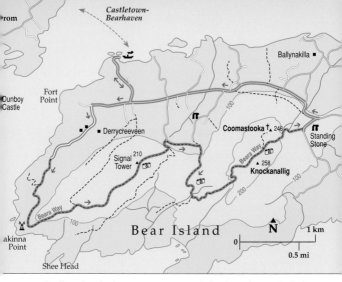

easterly direction before veering northeast onto the SUMMIT with the ruined signal tower (**1h53min**). This was one of a chain of towers built along Ireland's west coast during the Napoleonic Wars. Unfortunately, this tower was struck by lightning in 1959 and finally blew down in 1964. Now head downhill in an easterly to northeasterly direction, towards the highest rise on the island. Meet a track at POST NO 24 and turn left (**2h**). Leave it in the next left bend (POST NO 25) and fork right on a minor path. Cross boggy ground, pass a fenced-off area on the left, and climb the opposite hillside to reach POST NO 26. Follow the contour of the hill along a stone wall to POST NO 27, where you meet a track (**2h08min**) and turn right uphill.

After crossing the ridge, the track descends, affording a good view over the remote boggy south of the island.

Keep left when the track forks at POST NO 28 (**2h34min**). You gradually ascend to a saddle between the twin peaks, Coomastooka to the left, topped with a white cross, and Knockanallig to the right (**3h07min**). A splendid view opens up over the east of the island — to the village of Rerrin and a Martello tower cresting the brow of a hill in the middle distance. Off the coast, some bigger ships lie in the sheltered waters of Bear Haven.

Cross a stile by an iron gate near POST NO 32 and meet a small asphalt road (**3h17min**). Notice the standing stone on the top of the hill opposite. Turn left downhill to a road junction, where you turn left again. Keep left at the next junction not long afterwards. Now stay ahead on the main road past any turn-offs for the next 40 minutes, before turning right down to the harbour (**4h05min**), regaining the PIER (**4h15min**).

Walk 6: GLEN INCHAQUIN

Distance: 3.8km/2.4mi; 1h20min
Grade: easy, with a climb of 170m/560ft along well-defined paths and tracks. Suitable at any time of the year and for people of all ages.
Equipment: sturdy shoes, water, optional picnic
How to get there and return: 🚌 to/from the last house at Glen Inchaquin (the 141km/ 88mi-point in Car tour 5). There is a charge for parking and using the very pleasant amenity area.

Glen Inchaquin is a long valley in unspoilt surroundings, with a succession of beautiful lakes along the valley floor. A spectacular waterfall tumbles down the steep rock face at the head of the valley. This lovely circular walk takes you past a secluded lake and along mountain paths over the upper end of the waterfall. You enjoy marvellous views over the lakes, green meadows and deciduous woodlands of the valley, towards Kenmare River bay, framed by the distant hills of the Iveragh Peninsula.

From the car park at the house at **Glen Inchaquin, start out** by heading down the track to the lower car park, where there are picnic tables and benches. Cross the mountain stream in the valley on stepping stones or by the log bridge (**5min**). From here there is a fine view of the waterfall, tumbling down the steep rock face — most impressive on a wet day. Cross a small arm of the stream almost at once and follow the gravel track uphill. Secluded **Lough Cummeenadillure** comes into view on the right, between the hills (**30min**). The track swings left uphill and

Lake Inchaquin (top) and the typical boggy terrain encountered on this walk

Inchaquin Waterfall

narrows to a path; RED-AND-WHITE IRON POLES now indicate the route. Some rocky outcrops afford a magnificent view to the northwest over the lakeland area. The path continues to ascend through bog and is cut into the turf layer in places. You reach a wooden sign indicating a short detour to the right for a great view of **Cummeenaloughaun** (**55min**). Situated in a high moorland valley, this isolated mountain lake supplies the waterfall.

Return to the main route and continue to the UPPER END OF THE WATERFALL, where a log bridge spans the stream (**1h**). Skirt a fenced-off area to the left before descending steps carved into the rock, enjoying a lovely view over Glen Inchaquin towards the Kenmare River. Soon pass through an iron gate (please close it after you) and walk down the grassy track. A picnic spot with just one table and a bench affords a particularly beautiful view of the valley (**1h 10min**; Picnic 5c); hopefully it is still free!

Some charcoal pits scar the slope down to the left; they testify to past clear-cutting of these woodlands. Up until the 17th century, this whole valley would have been cloaked in aboriginal forest. Nowadays just Uragh Wood is left, a predominantly oak-filled nature reserve extending along the southwestern shores of Lough Inchaquin.

The track gradually veers to the left and draws nearer to a chattering stream with cascades and rock pools — these make ideal spots for bathing on a warm summer's day.

Further down in the valley, you pass through two iron gates in quick succession, before you join the main track. Turn left along it. Soon you will see signs for a river walk. *Do* take this, as it makes a delightful end; then return to where you left the car, at the last house in **Glen Inchaquin** (**1h20min**).

Walk 7: MUCKROSS AND THE KILLARNEY NATIONAL PARK

See also photographs on pages 36 and 102
Distance: 12.6km/7.8mi; 3h45min
Grade: moderate, with a climb of 80m/260ft. The walk mostly follows a small asphalt lane.
Equipment: walking boots, wind/waterproof jacket, water, picnic
How to get there and return: 🚌 to/from a car park on the

N71. From the roundabout in Killarney town centre take the main N71 south, signposted to Muckross House and Gardens. Pass the right turn to Ross Castle, cross the river Flesk and continue for another 2.8km/ 1.7mi to a small car park on the right (about 9.1km/5.7mi from the town centre); there are usually some jaunting cars waiting here (Car tour 6).

Killarney National Park is the most popular lakeland in Ireland. Ancient woods of oaks and yews surround the lakes and cloak the hillsides. Lough Leane's vast expanse of water is dotted with tiny islands, while smaller Muckross Lake is overlooked by densely-wooded Torc Mountain. This lovely walk takes you from the idyllic Muckross Friary, set close to the shore of Lough Leane, past Muckross Lake to romantic Dinish Cottage, before ascending the steep slopes of Torc Mountain. The Muckross Gardens are a sheer delight, with a great variety of exotic shrubs and trees. Last but not least, Muckross House is a beautiful 19th-century Elizabethan Revival manor house open to the public. *Do* make an early start to have the friary and the lake all to yourself!

Start out at the CAR PARK ON THE N71: go through the black iron gate and follow the tarred lane into the park, with Muckross Friary coming into view on the right. Turn right into an old avenue of towering lime and chesnut trees called the Friars' Walk and follow it to the ruin of **Muckross Friary**, pleasantly situated on the wooded shore of **Lough Leane** (**5min**). Note the huge yew tree in the cloisters, said to be more than 800 years old. There is a nice view across the graveyard out over the island-studded lake.
Return through the avenue and turn right on the tarred lane. Pass the first fork on your

left, but turn left at the next junction, signposted to Muckross House and Gardens. This tarred lane runs through **Monks' Wood** with its exotic shrubs and trees. Fork right as you emerge from the wood and Lough Leane comes into view again, following signs to Dinish Cottage and the Meeting of the Waters. Keep straight ahead at the junction by a pretty cottage on your left, and pass **Arthur Vincent House** on the right almost immediately (**30min**).
The tarred lane emerges from the wood and continues through a swampy area. Notice Torc Mountain towering ahead of you to the left as you

approach **Muckross Lake**. A short grassy path leads down to the peaceful water's edge, where you can sit on a wooden bench and relax (**55min**). The densely-wooded slopes of Torc look quite impassable from here, and there is no trace of the path traversing them. The tarred lane continues through mixed woodland with ancient oaks, yews and hollies. You'll see strawberry trees as well — one of the Lusitanian plants native to Ireland's mild southwest, but more commonly associated with Portugal or southwestern France. Its edible but rather tasteless fruits bear some

Meeting of the Waters

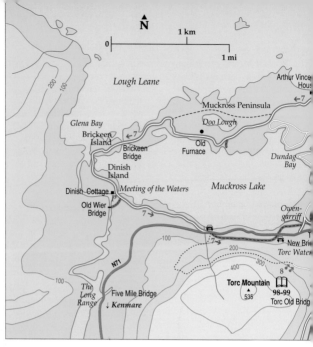

resemblance to strawberries. You pass a small sandy cove down on the left and soon reach the **Old Furnace** on the right, a ruined building with ivy-clad walls. Despite its name it has nothing to do with smelting works, but was more likely a summer house on the Muckross estate. Some ruined houses and pits are seen on both sides of the lane — remnants from the days of copper smelting in the 18th century.

At the end of the Muckross Peninsula you cross over to **Brickeen Island** via a hump-backed bridge (**1h25min**), with the waters of Muckross to the left and Lough Leane to the right. Continue along the causeway round the western tip of Muckross Lake, passing imperceptibly on to **Dinish Island**. Here you come upon idyllic **Dinish Cottage** (**1h45min**; Picnic 6a), surrounded by exotic plants including eucalyptus,

Californian redwoods, and camellias. You can sit on the wooden benches and enjoy your own picnic — or buy refreshments in high season. Another lovely place to take a break is by the **Meeting of the Waters** at the rear of the cottage gardens, where the waters from the Upper Lake divide to flow round Dinish Island. Just upstream, the picturesque Old Weir Bridge arches over the rapids. Continuing along the tarred lane, cross a small bridge almost immediately and go through an iron gate. Just beyond it, watch for a sign-posted path forking right into the trees; this short side-trip (partly on a boardwalk and waymarked with white and red posts) takes you to the **Old Weir Bridge**. Continue along the tarred lane to skirt Muckross Lake through more woodland full of oak and Scots pines.

You reach a car park alongside

Torc Waterfall

the main N71 (**2h10min**). Cross the road and follow the footpath opposite. It bends to the left, running parallel with the road along the lower slopes of **Torc Mountain** before leading back to the N71. Crossing the main road, continue on the pleasant woodland path. Pass a farmstead and go left downhill by the wooden gate, to cross an old stone bridge over the **Owengarriff River**. On meeting a tarred lane almost immediately, turn right uphill. Reach the **Torc New Bridge** and go through the short tunnel to the right that takes you under the main road. Then go past the national park display building and follow the pleasant footpath upstream, with the river on your right tumbling boisterously down over rocks and pools, to arrive at the foot of the **Torc Waterfall**, cascading down a steep boulder-strewn ravine (**2h50min**). By now you will

no doubt have come upon hoards of tourists ... and for the rest of the walk there will be no escape, unless you've picked a rainy day in mid-winter!

Retrace your steps from the waterfall. When you emerge from the tunnel under the main N71, cross the tarred lane and keep ahead on the gravel path. Entering the grounds of the **Muckross Estate**, follow the path across open parkland. Bear right at a fork, following the footpath along the edge of the wood. Entering the wood, go over a small wooden bridge, and soon go through an iron gate. When you see a majestic Monterey cypress, turn left across the tarred lane, to visit the **Dundag Boathouses** — one wet for ready use and one dry for long-term storage. Return to the cypress and turn left on the gravel path to continue. Now wander at

97

Jaunting cars near Killarney

leisure through the arboretum, marvelling at the great varity of exotic plants flourishing in these well-kept gardens. You will eventually come to **Muckross House** at the northern end of the arboretum; walk round it to the front entrance (**3h25min**). From the house follow the main entrance driveway straight through the open parkland, to reach a small crossroads after a couple of minutes. Turn right and stay ahead on this lane past any forks. When you come to the upper end of **Friars' Walk** at the top of the hill, turn left down through the lovely avenue. Turn right on meeting a tarred lane and return to the CAR PARK ON THE N71 (**3h45min**).

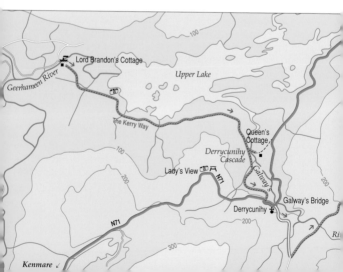

Walk 8: FROM LORD BRANDON'S COTTAGE ALONG OLD KENMARE ROAD TO MUCKROSS HOUSE

See also photos on the cover, pages 36, 95 and opposite; map continues on page 96
Distance: 15km; 4h30min
Grade: moderate, with a climb of 310m/1029ft overall. This walk follows the waymarked Kerry Way. Suitable all year round, but some sections of the walk are prone to flooding after heavy and persistent rain; enquire locally before setting on the walk..
Equipment: walking boots, wind-/waterproof jacket, water, picnic
How to get there and return: 🚌 to Ross Castle. From the centre of Killarney head south on the N71. Almost immediately, turn right at the first petrol station on the right. This minor road leads after

2km to the big car park at Ross Castle (Car tour 6 at 2.9km). Park here, then follow the short signposted footpath to the jetty where the boats depart. ⛴ Boats leave every day at 10am; check the departure time and arrive in time, and *don't forget that you only want to pay for a one-way trip*. It's a good idea to make a booking on the previous evening: Killarney Boating Centre, High Street, phone 064 31068. The walk ends at Muckross House, from where you can take a jaunting car or a taxi back to the car park at Ross Castle. This restored tower house, seat of the O'Donoghues, can be visited either at the beginning or the end of the walk.

$\mathbf{A}$fter a lovely boat trip taking an hour and a half, this magnificent walk takes you from Lord Brandon's Cottage along the Old Kenmare Road back to Killarney. The boat trip from Ross Castle across the

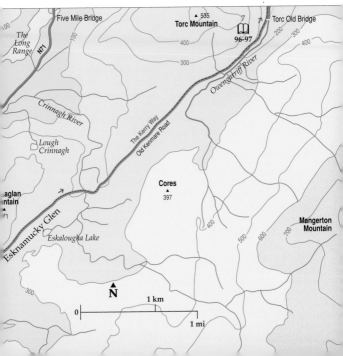

wide expanse of Lough Leane and smaller Muckross Lake runs via Dinish Island (Walk 7), from where the boats pass under the Old Weir Bridge. The water flow is so strong at this romantic two-arched stone bridge that the boats have to be towed upstream. Beyond the bridge the landscape begins to open up again. The boats navigate through The Long Range to the peaceful Upper Lake, where Lord Brandon's Cottage sits near the Gearhameen River at the western lakeshore, over-looking the lake from its high round tower. Lord Brandon, a wealthy clergyman, built the house as his country seat at the beginning of the 19th century, but only the original stables remain.

Start out at **Lord Brandon's Cottage** by turning left at the junction in front of the restaurant, ignoring the path signposted for the 'Black Valley'. The footpath you are on runs some distance from the **Upper Lake**; boardwalks lead across some waterlogged sections. There are lovely views on your left across the Upper Lake dotted with small islets. The background is filled by Macgillycuddy's Reeks (Walk 9), the highest mountain range in Ireland.

The path runs through lovely mixed woodland with oaks, holly, yews and strawberry trees, not to forget the ubiquitous rhododendrons with their mauve-coloured flowers shimmering in spring between the surrounding lush greenery. Reach a fork where the walk will continue to the right uphill, but first keep left on the main path for a short detour. The path passes below an abandoned house surrounded by fuchsias and big rhododendrons before leading down to river flats. A wooden footbridge crosses **Galway's River** at **Derrycunihy Cascade**, where the water gushes down between boulders. Continue to follow

the path beyond the bridge for a short section until you can see **Queen's Cottage** up on your right (**50min**), where Queen Victoria stayed overnight on her visit to Ireland.

Return the same way to the fork and turn sharp left. The small path winds uphill through the lovely wood. Climb some stone steps; occasional boardwalks lead across waterlogged sections. When you reach the MAIN ROAD (N71), turn left. On your left you can see **Galway's Bridge** with its beautiful stone arches spanning the river, while on the right is **Derry-cunihy Church** (also called Old Church; **1h20min**), a picturesque but somewhat neglected building. Leave the main road here and go straight ahead past the church on the asphalted field track. Impres-sive rhododendrons stand by the wayside, a beautiful sight when they are in blossom. The track swings to the left, then to the right, before leading through a plain where turf is cut. You are surrounded by wild hills; a lonely house sits at the foot of the hillside oppo-site. The track crosses a small arched bridge. Just 75m/yds further on, at a signpost, turn left on the footpath.

Gradually climbing, you pass through an enchanted oak wood where in misty weather dwarfs and fairies may still be glimpsed between the trees. Moss-covered ruins by the side of the path testify to earlier settlements — before the people living here were relocated by their landlord. Cross **Galway's River** on a wooden footbridge in an open area (**1h45min**), then climb more steeply beside mossy stone walls through the oaks. You are following the **Old Kenmare Road** — the main road between Killarney and Kenmare before the N71 was built. The old road and the entire area between Mangerton Mountain and the lakes of Killarney were closed in the 1830s, when the landowner at the time, H A Herbert, decided this should be his private hunting ground. The farmers had to move, and he even had Old Torc Bridge demolished, to make sure nobody could use the old road any more.

Eventually you leave the trees behind. Rocky hills rise on the right, while to the left Macgillycuddy's Reeks can be seen in the distance. Pass a shed with a collapsed rusty-red iron roof on the right. Soon a long section of boardwalk leads through a waterlogged area. Along this section the original route of the Old Kenmare Road is no longer visible. Surrounded by desolate hills, the path leads you over hedge and ditch; boardwalks take you through particularly muddy places.

Ahead on your right you'll catch a glimpse of little **Eskalougha Lake**. Head back into the trees and follow the old cobbled trail along a small river through long **Esknamucky Glen** (**2h25min**). Travelling from Kenmare to Killarney in 1776, Arthur Young thought this area 'the wildest and most romantic country' — and little has changed since. The rocky glen is graced by beautiful oaks, birches and holly. It remains a mystery, however, how horse-drawn carts could have ever driven along such routes. Further downhill the glen opens up to a flat plain which was once covered by a lake; now the Crinnagh River winds through it. A gravel path takes you through these muddy, reed-covered flats. A small waterfall called **Core's Cascade** plummets down on your right over dark basalt rock. The path winds its way along the **Crinnagh River** and crosses it on a small footbridge. The landscape is dotted by strange stone humps which could easily be mistaken for megalithic buildings ... but the reality is more prosaic: they are just stones piled up from land clearance.

At the end of the plain you reach the beginning of a gravel track. Its former stone cobbles are still visible in places. This track ascends initially, then runs straight through flat open moorland. **Mangerton Mountain**, at 839m/2750ft the highest peak in the area, rises on the right, while **Torc Mountain** (535m/1755ft) is seen ahead on the left. On your right, the Owengarriff River winds its way through marshland. At the foot of Torc Mountain the track leads into the shady forest.

Muckross House (Walks 7 and 8)

Continue straight ahead past a right turn that leads across a wooden footbridge (**Torc Old Bridge**), keeping on the left side of the valley. Shortly after passing a left turn, fork sharp right on a stony track, down to the bridge over the **Owengarriff River** (**3h50min**). Cross the bridge and, 50m/yds further on, bear left at a track junction, passing a big mossy beech tree on the right. Follow this beautiful path downhill while listening to the pleasant sound of running water from the wooded valley below. Soon you reach the viewing platform at **Torc Waterfall** (**3h55min**) where you are all of a sudden in the midst of the crowds. The waterfall cascades down some 20m/60ft over sandstone rocks into the green valley. *Walk 7 joins here; refer to the map on pages 96-97.* Descend the path along the river, ignoring the car park on the right, and go straight through a short tunnel under the main road (**Torc New Bridge**). Beyond it, cross an asphalt lane and continue straight ahead on the gravel path. There is a sweeping view over a green lawn dotted with grazing cows all the way to Muckross Lake.

Bear right at a fork, following the footpath along the edge of the wood. Entering the wood, go over a small wooden bridge, and soon go through an iron gate. Near a giant Monterey cypress the path approaches an asphalt lane on the left. Follow the signpost here, to take make a short detour to the nearby **Dundag Boathouses** (**4h20min**) at the shore of **Muckross Lake**. Then return to the cypress and continue on the gravel path leading into the arboretum. Lovingly laid out, **Muckross Gardens** are a sheer delight; there is a great variety of exotic shrubs and trees. To the north of the arboretum is **Muckross House** (**4h30min**), a beautiful 19th-century Elizabethan Revival manor house open to the public. Just in front of the main door is the departure point of the jaunting cars that will take you back to **Ross Castle** where you started the walk. You could also extend the walk by continuing to **Muckross Friary**, pleasantly situated on the wooded shore of **Lough Leane**, and taking a jaunting car from there. But I don't recommend walking back to Ross Castle on foot: it's 5km along the main road.

Walk 9: CARRAUNTOOHIL, THE HIGHEST MOUNTAIN IN IRELAND

Distance: 12.1km/7.6mi; 5h15min

Grade: strenuous, with an ascent/descent of 910m/ 3000ft. Take this walk very seriously. The extremely steep and slippery climb up the notorious Devil's Ladder should only be tackled by experienced mountain walkers. You must be sure-footed. *Do not attempt this hike if there is even the remotest chance of bad weather.* In rainy weather the Devil's Ladder becomes a waterfall and the Gaddagh River cannot be forded on the stepping stones. The Short walk below is ideal for less agile walkers.

Equipment: walking boots, warm wind/waterproof jacket, walking stick, water, picnic; compass an advantage

How to get there and return: 🚌 to/from the parking area at Cronin's Yard (Car tour 6, page 38). Leave the Killarney-

Killorglin road (N72) by turning south across Beaufort Bridge to Beaufort. Follow the main road straight ahead past the Beaufort Bar. Keep straight on, ignoring a right turn signposted to a church. You pass interesting ogham stones on the left, cross a small bridge and keep right at the fork just beyond it. Reach a staggered crossroads, where you turn right past the road signposted for the Gap of Dunloe and Black Valley. Keep straight on at another crossroads with a small petrol station on the right. Some 150m further on, take the signposted left turn to Cronin's Yard. This small road ascends past some houses and affords good views over the Gaddagh Valley. Keep straight ahead to Cronin's Yard (www.croninsyard.com, tel: 064-34936; showers, WC, telephone box) at the end of

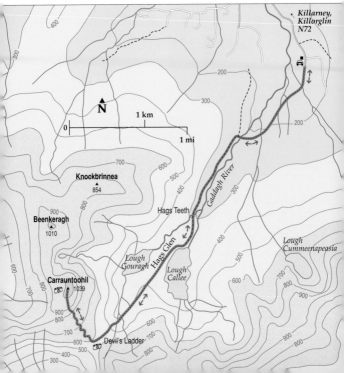

the road (nominal parking fee). **Short walk: Hags Glen.** Follow the main walk to Hags Glen and turn back there (6.3km/3.9mi; 2h05min return; easy, with an ascent of 200m/655ft; access and equipment as above).

At 1039m/3408ft, Carrauntoohil (in Gaelic *Corrán Tuathail*; 'sickle; serrated mountain'), is the highest point in Ireland. It rises up from Macgillycuddy's Reeks (*Na Cruacha Dubha*; 'the steep black hills') — the wild mountain range between the Gap of Dunloe in the east and Lough Acoose in the west that dominates much of the Iveragh Peninsula. This walk follows the classic route up to the summit via the Devil's Ladder, a steep rubble-strewn gully. You will be rewarded for the strenuous ascent by magnificent panoramic views from the summit.

Start out at the FARMYARD and follow the well-trodden grassy trail past the iron gate. Soon you reach FOUR IRON GATES: go through the one on the left. Cross a stream on a concrete FOOTBRIDGE (**3min**), beyond which the trail becomes more obvious and stonier underfoot. Pass a concrete construction and a stone marker inscribed 'SV' on the left, then cross another stream on STEPPING STONES (**23min**). About 100m/yds further on, watch for a white arrow painted on a rock and follow it to the right — don't take the route straight up. Soon cross the **Gaddagh River** on boulders strewn in the riverbed (**28min**); this may take some time depending on the water level and your agility. Climb straight uphill for about 50m/yds, towards another stone marker inscribed 'WM', before swinging left on the stony and grassy trail that ascends along the slope. Soon emerging on a track, follow it to the left (almost straight ahead). This track is much

Top: Macgillycuddy's Reeks; left: brook in Hags Glen

easier underfoot. It runs parallel with the Gaddagh River, which is cut deeply into the scree on the left. The steep ridge ahead of you rises to the right, towards the summit of Carrauntoohil. The cross atop this cone-shaped mountain should be discernible from here. If not, the visibility may be too poor for you to be able to tackle the climb. Pass a short concrete chute on the right. At **Hags Teeth** you turn left across the Gaddagh River on stepping stones (**1h**).

The wide stony track climbs towards the amphitheatre of steep rocky slopes ahead, known as **Hags Glen**. Wild and romantic **Lough Callee** appears on the left, as the track reduces to a trail. Here you come upon a large cairn on the right-hand side of the trail (**1h15min**). *(This marks the point where the Short walk turns back.)*

Leaving the lake on the left, continue on the fairly faint trail (now marked by cairns). The surrounding escarpments gradually close in, with **Lough Gouragh** coming into sight down on the right. When the cairned trail finally peters out, maintain a more or less straight course towards the foot of the rock and scree gully called the Devil's Ladder. Pick the best dry line you can find to traverse the boggy basin at the head of the valley, avoiding soft ground. Here again, take your time to cross this waterlogged area of mountain streams and rocky outcrops.

When you reach the lower end of the **Devil's Ladder** at the head of the valley (**2h**), you are facing the most difficult part of the walk. It runs almost vertically up the rocky escarpment. The scramble looks frightening from this point, but you will soon find (with great relief) that it is less demanding and vertiginious than expected. Climb the scree gully, taking great care on loose stones and rocks. After rain, water will be coming down, so *extra care* is needed. As you scramble carefully up, stop occasionally to look back down over Hags Glen with the two lakes.

At the upper end of the Devil's Ladder you emerge on a wind-swept grassy SADDLE (**2h45min**). Get your breath back and enjoy the magnificent views on both sides. From here several cairned routes lead up the rocky hillside on the right; just follow the main one. A large metal cross by a small stone enclosure marks the SUMMIT of **Carrauntoohil** (**3h45min**) where, on a clear day, there are unsurpassed panoramic views of the entire Iveragh Peninsula and most of Kerry.

Now return the way you came via the Devil's Ladder and past Lough Callee. Watch for your faint turn-off right some 15 minutes after the concrete chute, where you have to leave the track. Cross the Gaddagh River again and follow your outward trail back to the car park at the FARMYARD (**5h15min**).

Walk 10: DERRYNANE

Distance: 8.3km/5.2mi; 2h40min

Grade: easy-moderate circular walk, with a climb of 150m/490ft. Suitable all year round, but the rocky coastal trail can be slippery in wet weather.

Equipment: walking boots or sturdy shoes, wind/waterproof jacket, water, picnic

How to get there and return: 🚗 to/from the car park at Derrynane House near Caherdaniel (the 81km/50mi-point on Car tour 6).

NB: Sand dunes are a very delicate habitat which can easily be damaged. Please stay on the path where it exists.

Derrynane *(Doire Fhionnán* or 'Finian's oak grove' in Gaelic) is an area of mixed woodland, marshes, sandy beaches, rock pools and dunes on the south coast of the Iveragh Peninsula. Surrounded by lovely gardens and parkland hosting a wide variety of exotic plants, Derrynane House is the ancestral home of Daniel O'Connell (1775-1847), the 'The Liberator', one of the most important politicians in Irish history. The house is open to the public and can be visited on self-guided tours.

Start out at the car park at **Derrynane House**: cross the road, ignoring the entrance to the house itself. Follow the track to the left (signposted 'Strand 100m'), going through the iron gate. Continue to the back of the dunes, before veering left on the path towards a rock outcrop known as **Altar Hill**. Pass the **Mass Rock** on the left and continue straight ahead, to head towards the shore of the estuary. Turn right on the path that runs alongside posts and wire fencing at the back of the dunes. When the path emerges on the SANDY BEACH (**20min**), turn right again and walk along it. (Swimming is not allowed here due to dangerous currents.)

At the end of the beach, pass some rocks jutting out into the water, climb the sandy embankment and continue straight ahead along the back of the next beach. Turn right at the end of it (where a wooden

106

holiday home sits atop a rock), to join the car park road. Turn left here, up to the main road. Then go left again and continue to the car park above **Derrynane Quay**, where the road ends (**45min**). Here you can make a short detour to the left along the beach or across the dunes to **Abbey Island**, where you come upon a graveyard with a small ruined church that dates back to the 10th century.

Return to the car park and walk towards the two houses opposite. Just about 25m/yds to the right of the left-hand house, go through a small gap in the stone wall. Here you join a path that runs towards a telephone pole. This old **Mass Path** snakes its way through the rocks above the coast. If you come here in July or August you will be delighted by myriads of orange-blooming montbretia. Soon you pass a stone boathouse built in 2004. The path then

takes you out onto a tiny beach, sadly littered. Cross it to the far end, then climb rough steps cut into the rocks on the right to continue on the path as it winds through coastal heath. Ignore all paths turning off left or right. This is the natural habitat of the rare Kerry lily *(Simethis planifolia)*, a protected plant on the verge of extinction. The path eventually joins a track near the entrance gate to an estate. Turn left and follow it straight ahead past a small beach on the left to **Bealtra Quay** (**1h20min**).

Continue along the asphalt road as it winds up past the occasional house. Fine coastal views begin to unfold, with the western tip of the Beara Peninsula seen in the distance. Turn right when you reach a T-junction, to continue climbing through rural countryside with stone-walled fields and some traditional farmhouses. Ignore a sharp turn on the left, but leave the asphalt road in a sharp hairpin bend to the left: fork right on a tarmac lane that contours along the hillside (**1h55min**). The tarmac ends at a gate; go through it or use the stile beside it, then continue on the track. Just 200m/yds past the gate, the poles of an electricity line run uphill to the left. Follow them up on a path across heath that

View to Abbey Island and the ruined 10th-century church

can be quite waterlogged after rain. Keep straight on to the TOP OF THE HILL, marked by a large flat stone — a perfect picnic spot (**2h15min**).

Stay ahead on the path as it descends the far side of the hill. Then the path bends to the right and runs down towards a stone wall. Keep left alongside the wall and descend through mixed woodland. On meeting an asphalt road, turn right and descend through woodland. Keep right at the first road junction. When you reach another junction, further downhill, turn left through **Bell Gate** (there's a bell in its arched pillar). Follow the lane past lovely gardens full of exotic plants. *Do* take time to explore the gardens before turning right to **Derrynane House** (**2h35min**). After your visit, walk straight down the main driveway back to the CAR PARK (**2h40min**).

Walk 11: FROM WATERVILLE ROUND LOUGH CURRANE

See photograph on page 38
Distance: 21.4km/13.3mi;
6h15min
Grade: moderate, but long,
with an overall ascent of 290m/
950ft. Suitable all year round;
some sections can be muddy
and waterlogged after rain.

Equipment: walking boots,
wind-/waterproof jacket,
water, picnic
How to get there and return:
🚌 to/from Waterville, on the
N70 (Ring of Kerry; the
97km-point on Car tour 6)
Park on the village esplanade.

Located on the Ring of Kerry at the southern end of the Iveragh Pensinsula, Waterville is a typical Victorian seaside resort. This circular walk follows small roads and old paths around a lake just behind beautiful Ballinskelligs Bay. En route you visit a small abandoned hamlet nestling on lush green hillsides.

Start out by leaving
Waterville on the main road
(N70) south and cross the
Currane River on an old
stone bridge. Fishing boats are
moored upstream between the
tall reeds by the river's edge.
These reeds *(Phragmites australis)* are the tallest native
grasses in Ireland. They can
grow up to four metres high;

in autumn they produce
decorative flower stalks. Not
far beyond the bridge turn left
on a minor asphalt road with
various signposts (Museum/
Heritage Centre and B&Bs).
This road passes several
wooded properties; on the left
is the former Club Med
complex by the shore of the
lake. The shady stone walls

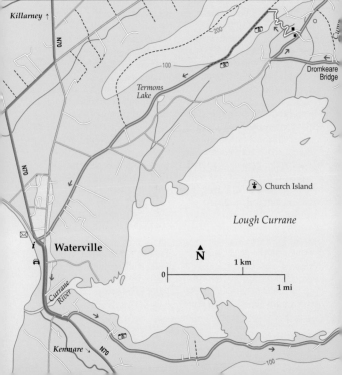

lining the road are covered with different ferns such as *Polypodium vulgare* and *Phyllitis scolopendrium* with its leathery, tongue-shaped leaves.

When you leave the dense woodland behind, there is a sweeping view over **Lough Currane**'s wide expanse of water. Its Gaelic name is *Loch Luíoch* ('Lake in the Lowland'). Legend has it that this lake was originally created by torrential rains. The Druids of a legendary Celtic tribe called *Tuatha Dé Danann* are said to have brought about this tremendous thunderstorm in order to destroy the Sons of Milesius invading Ireland around 1300 BC. Most of the invaders drowned in the raging torrents.

The road approaches the shore. In the middle of the lake, small Church Island can be seen, with the ruins of a 12th-century monastery. Gradually you get closer to the hills rising inland, passing through dense woods with oaks and hazel. Once again the lake is in view.

Eventually you leave the asphalt road and turn left onto the signposted track of the **Kerry Way**, which you will now follow for a while. Cross the **Capall River** on a concrete bridge (**2h**) and follow the track into the conifers. Leave the conifers behind; oaks and holly are now seen growing beside the route. A small marshy valley with a brook runs on the right. The stony hillsides were once cultivated but are now covered with heath and ferns. Called **Cloghvoola** ('stony milking place'), this region was more densely populated in the past, but now there are just two farms still inhabited.

When you reach a track junction, fork sharp left uphill, passing through an iron gate with stile ('Private — no through road') and climbing up the track. The views over the Cloghvoola area steadily improve as you ascend. Keep following the YELLOW/BLACK POSTS AND ARROWS of the Kerry Way, gradually making your way uphill. The waymarking posts and arrows eventually lead you across the next trackless stretch of waterlogged hillside. Soon you're walking on the middle of a ridge, enjoying a magnificent view of the bay near Waterville and Bolus Head. At the nose of the ridge a post points you sharply to the right. Descend to a cattle fence and walk alongside it. Soon cross a stile and continue ahead, gradually descending a grassy, partly waterlogged path

Lined by hedges, this lane at first runs dead straight, before eventually crossing the **Cummeragh River** via old **Dromkeare Bridge** (**4h15min**) and rising in a double bend. Then the lane runs straight to a crossroads where you turn right. Follow the road for the next five minutes, until you reach a cottage on the left set back from the road and surrounded by conifers. Turn left just past this enclosure, on a track ascending the wooded hillside. *(Please note this is a private track; do respect the landowner.)*

Pass a house on the right and continue uphill, going through an iron gate almost immediately. Soon climb over another iron gate and reach an old GRASSY TRACK (**5h05min**). Follow this to the left along the hillside, enjoying a magnificent view of Lough Currane with Church Island in its middle. On the far side of the lake the treeless hilltops of Mullaghbeg (509m) and Cahernageeha Mountain (499m) can be seen. As you walk along the track you have to negotiate two more iron gates before passing an old abandoned cottage. Now continue straight ahead, gradually downhill, via more iron gates. At the first inhabited house the track becomes asphalt. Follow this road straight ahead past the occasional house, until you reach a crossroads. Here turn right and walk back along the road to **Waterville** (**6h15min**).

straight along the hillside. After a short while the path descends through a small rocky gully, running with water after rain. Yellow arrows on some rocks indicate your route. Then the path runs through a flat muddy area. Watch out for the posts of the Kerry Way.

The path becomes wider, leading past some stone walls and approaching the houses of **Cahersavane** (**3h40min**). At the first farm, turn right on a track. Up on the fern-clad hillside a beautiful ring-fort is visible between stone walls covered with white lichen. Following the level track, you pass an iron gate with stile and meet a T-junction where you leave the Kerry Way by turning left on the lane.

Walk 12: ANASCAUL

Distance: 6.4km/4mi; 2h30min

Grade: easy, with a climb of 300m/985ft. Suitable at any time of the year, unless it is misty or the cloud cover is low. The route can be waterlogged in its upper section.

Equipment: walking boots, wind/waterproof jacket, water, picnic

How to get there and return: 🚗 to/from the lakeside car park *before reaching* Anascaul (the 28km/17mi-point on Car tour 7). Turn left at the western entrance to Anascaul village (just before crossing the bridge), following signs for Annascaul Lake. Keep straight ahead to reach a crossroads, where you turn right. Continue past a fork to the left and another one to the right. Drive through two iron gates down to the lakeside car park (3.8km/2.4mi from Anascaul).

Enclosed by precipitous slopes, peaceful Lough Anascaul *(Loch an Scáil)* lies in a magnificent glen. From the upland heath, a river rushes down through this wild and secluded valley, cascading over rocks in its upper reaches. This walk follows a good track from the lake to the high moors and back down the same way.

Start out at the CAR PARK overlooking **Lough Anascaul** and follow the track that leads into the glen. Across the lake, bare scree-slopes rise steeply to the towering cliffs of **Dromavally**, while the equally precipitous **Carrigblagher Cliffs** rise to your left. Go through an iron gate and stay ahead on the track as it follows the course of the **Garrivagh River** that feeds the lake. You'll notice a large cuboid boulder on your left, an ancient 'mass rock', used by the people for celebrating mass at a time when Catholicism was still supressed. On the 17th of August every year, mass is still

Mt Brandon from the Connor Pass (Car tour 7)

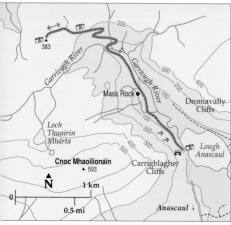

Anascaul Lake, backed by the steep-sided scree slopes of Dromavally

celebrated here to commemorate the past, when rocks had to serve as makeshift altars.

Go through another iron gate and continue to climb more steeply on the stony, sometimes eroded track. The river rushes noisily down below you on the right and tumbles over a gushing WATERFALL (**40min**). Soon turn right across a small concrete bridge over the river. The track begins to deteriorate as it ascends; this old bog road is now quite waterlogged and eroded in places. Another small concrete bridge is crossed a couple of minutes later, just

112

before the route swings left. Beyond a third bridge the old bog road, now overgrown with rushes, ascends in two more zigzags to the hilltop. Looking back, you have an ever-better view of the glaciated valley, with the still watersheet of Lough Anascaul down at the bottom. Leave the old road before it peters out in the high bog and head left uphill for about 300m/yds, to reach the OBVIOUS RISE (383m/1256ft; **1h30min**). From up here you enjoy a splendid view over the wild and untamed mountains around, all densely cloaked in heather, moorland grasses and moss. Steep-sided Mt Brandon, Ireland's second-highest peak, rises in the northwest.
Return the same way to the lakeside CAR PARK (**2h30min**).

Walk 13: MOUNT EAGLE

See also photograph on pages 40-41

Distance: 7.8km/4.9mi; 3h20min

Grade: moderate, with an ascent of 500m/1640ft overall. For the most part this circular walk follows well-defined tracks, but there is a steep cross-country section over boggy heath. Suitable at any time of the year, but choose a clear and hazeless day to enjoy the fine views. Do not attempt in misty weather or when there is a risk of low cloud.

Equipment: walking boots, wind/waterproof jacket, walking stick, water, picnic

How to get there and return: 🚌 There are two possibilities to get to the starting point. You can either follow the main R559 from Ventry (*Ceann Trá*; the 54km/34mi-point in Car tour 7) to the first crossroads beyond the village, marked by a church (Seipial Naom Caitliona) and a pub (Paidi O Se's). Turn right, following a sign for Dún Chaoin. Follow this small road straight ahead as it gradually

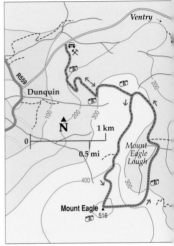

begins to climb the hill. After 4.6km/2.9mi along this road, a track branches off to the left; this is where the walk starts. Alternatively, complete the Slea Head Drive round Mount Eagle to Dunquin, then, where the road bends left, turn right on a small road signposted to *Ceann Trá* (Ventry). About 0.9km/0.6mi up this road, turn right on a track and park at the side of it.

Standing guard over Ireland's most westerly coastline, flat-topped Mount Eagle *(Sliabh an Iolair)* rises high above the sea at the end of the Dingle Peninsula. This splendid circular walk takes you along an old bog road to the top, before descending over high mountain heath down to a secluded tarn, superbly sited at the bottom of a steep-sided corrie. Magnificent views over the surrounding seascapes accompany you most of the way.

Set off following the track that runs straight uphill from the **Ventry road**, passing a left turn to a small abandoned quarry some 100m/yds along. As you climb, magnificent views begin to unroll. You look down the heathery slopes onto the green patchwork of fields covering the coastal plain, embroidered with the whitewashed cottages of Dunquin. Across Blasket Sound the distant Blasket Islands are a brilliant sight on a sunny day. Great Blasket *(An Blascaod Mór)* is the largest island, while Inishtooskert *(Inis*

113

Tuaisceart) — also known as Dead Man Island — is easily identified: from this angle its silhouette is reminiscent of a corpse lying in state.

The track zigzags up to a broad SHOULDER (**1h**), flattens out briefly, then swings right and ascends more gradually. As you proceed you enjoy glimpses of the bays of Ventry and Dingle in the east and Smerwick Harbour in the north behind you. The track leads to turf cuttings and peters out. Keep going straight across the cut turf banks, up the steep hillside. There is no distinct path, nor can you see the summit from here — so head straight up towards two adjacent standing stones. When you reach them, continue up to the flat-topped SUMMIT of **Mount Eagle**, marked by a concrete trig point (516m/1695ft; **1h50min**).

Enjoy the splendid panoramic views around you, extending over turf-laden hills, green coastal plains and remote islands dotting an indigo-blue sea. Mount Eagle is the most westerly rise in the mountain chain that forms the backbone of the Dingle Peninsula. Across Dingle Bay, the neighbouring Iveragh Peninsula rises in the south, while the Blasket Islands sprinkle the blue waters of the Atlantic in the west.

From the summit, head down to the left (due east) through boggy heath by walking in the direction of Ventry Harbour. Keep clear of the precipitous cliff on your left. Far below, Mount Eagle Lough is seen at the bottom of the steep-sided corrie. Follow the cliff-edge until the escarpment becomes less steep. Your next goal is the small pier at the northeastern end of the lake. Head straight down the boggy hillside, taking care on this steep descent, to reach the shore. Follow it round to the right to the small PIER (**2h20min**). With the pier at your back, note the rough overgrown track ahead of you to the left, running diagonally uphill. Head straight across the field to the bottom of this track and follow it uphill. It is little used and waterlogged in places, so keep to the drier margins. The track veers left near the end of the ascent, before meeting your OUTWARD TRACK on a bend (**2h50min**). Turn right to retrace your steps back to the **Ventry road** (**3h20min**).

View to Ventry and Dingle Harbour from Mt Eagle

Walk 14: THE BURREN

See also photographs page 45
Distance: 23km/14.4mi;
5h30min
Grade: quite strenuous due to
its length, with a moderate
climb of 590m/1935ft overall.
Agility, stamina and a good
sense of orientation required.
Do not attempt in misty
weather or when there is a risk
of low cloud; you need a fine
da to follow the route easily.
Equipment: walking boots,
wind/waterproof jacket,
walking stick, plenty of water,
picnic, adequate sun
protection; compass an
advantage
How to get there and return:
🚌 to/from the car park at
Fanore beach (the 50km/
31mi-point on Car tour 8).
Shorter walk: Caher Valley.
Take a shortcut back along the
road (19km/11.9mi, 4h30min;
moderate to strenuous, with an
ascent of 420m/1380ft overall;
equipment and access as
above). Follow the main walk
to the 3h30min-point, then
stay on the road through the
Caher Valley and follow it
straight down to the main road
at Fanore. Opposite is the track
you originally followed
through the colony of
caravans. Now retrace your
steps via Fanore beach back to
the car park.

Facing the Atlantic, the stark grey limestone terraces of The Burren (*Boireann;* 'rocky land' in Gaelic) are a world of their own. This intriguing karst landscape has a strange lunar-like appearance that can be quite forbidding on an overcast day. Deceptive in its barrenness, the Burren boasts rare plants growing in its countless crevices, with both alpine and warmth-loving species flourishing side by side. Below its scarred surface, a complex system of caves and subterranean waterways permeates the carboniferous massif. This fascinating landscape is now a national park, and there is no better way of exploring it than this invigorating circular walk.

Start out at the CAR PARK at **Fanore**: go down to the sandy beach and turn right along it. Cross the shallow **Murroogh River** and turn right immediately beyond it to leave the beach. When you reach the beginning of a track, follow it through a rather unsightly colony of caravans spread out in the dunes. Ignore a left turn but, when you come to the main road, turn left. Leave the main road after a few minutes and fork half-right on a gravel track through **Murroogh** (**30min**). When this track bends right towards the last houses, climb over the low stone wall ahead of you and continue on the old 'green road', keeping straight ahead. (There is dense scrub for the first few metres, but this short overgrown section can easily be avoided.) Beyond it the wide grassy trail reveals itself, walled on both sides, more or less following the contour of the hill.

Follow the green road high above **Black Head**, round the northwestern flank of **The Burren**; the lighthouse down

115

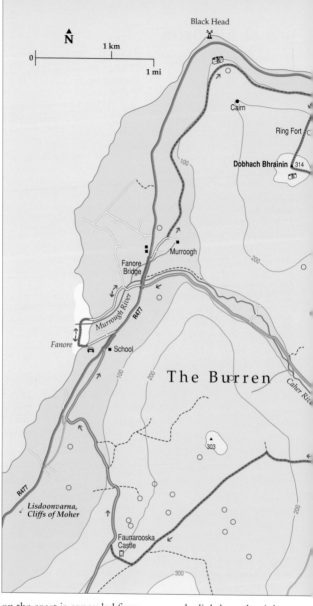

Black Head

Cairn

Ring Fort

Dobhach Bhrainin ▲ 314

Murroogh

Fanore
Bridge

Murrough River

R477

Fanore

School

The Burren

Caher Riv...

▲ 303

R477

*Lisdoonvarna,
Cliffs of Moher*

Faunarooska
Castle

300

on the coast is concealed from up here. Notice the big cairn on the hill to the right; it serves as a useful landmark. Just beyond a STONE WALL that crosses your way (the cairn is now well behind you up on the right; **1h50min**), the green road broadens briefly, then

ascends slightly to the right (red arrows), before petering out. Turn right at the stone wall and climb pathless straight up the hill.
Keep following the stone wall until the gradient eases. Your next landmark is a well-preserved RING-FORT to the left

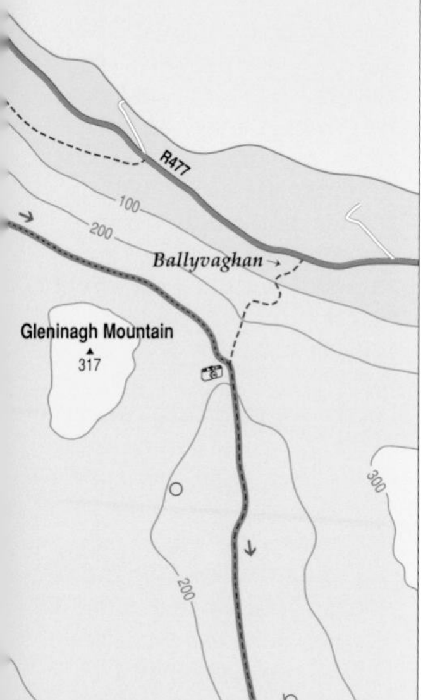

R477

100
200

Ballyvaghan →

Gleninagh Mountain
317

300

200

Burren Way

Slí Bhoirne

200

Rathborney River

of the stone wall: much of its outer wall remains intact (**1h15min**). Built by the Celts, such circular enclosures served as fortified farmsteads where the entire family plus their livestock would live side by side. On a windy day, you can shelter here and meditate how life might have been in centuries past.

Take great care on the following cross-country section over the rough limestone plateau and watch for the frequent crevices. Maintaining a straight course, head across the plateau and then straight up (some small cairns mark the best ascent) onto the flat summit of **Dobhach Bhrainin**. A mound of stones, or massive cairn that looks like a small stone tower, crowns the SUMMIT and helps locate the highest point on this fairly uniform elevation (314m/ 1030ft; **1h45min**). Enjoy sweeping views over the bare terraced limestone hills of the Burren and locate your next goal, flat-topped Gleninagh Mountain in the southeast. You are not going to climb Gleninagh, however; you will be circling round its left-hand slope by following the contour of the hill.

The obvious route to Gleninagh leads along a flat low-lying ridge skirting a great bowl on the right. Descending from the summit, initially aim for Galway Bay slightly to the left of Gleninagh. Cross a stone wall after a few minutes. Now aim for a stone wall further downhill, running in a southeasterly direction. Follow it as it contours along the flat ridge and then round the northern flank of **Gleninagh**. When a saddle opens up ahead, separating the mountain you are on from the opposite summit, your route begins to descend. You cross a stone wall, after which you continue straight down some 75m/yds to the top of the COL, where you meet a rough old trail (**2h15min**).

Follow its winding course

right (**3h30min**). Fork left almost immediately *(but carry straight on down the valley for the Shorter walk)* and cross a bridge over the **Caher River**. Fork right on the green road almost immediately and climb past an old cottage on your right (now used as a cowshed). You pass another ruined cottage on the right before negotiating a short overgrown section. Continue your ascent on the surprisingly-wide grassy trail between neat drystone walls.

Follow the green road round to the left where a minor trail continues straight ahead and keep climbing. When the ascent eases, the route takes you straight across a limestone plateau, with the shale summit of **Slieve Elva** rising to the south. You go through a number of iron gates before gradually beginning to descend. Pass a ruined house on the left and go through another iron gate. Leave the green road very soon, turning right along the second stone wall running down the hillside. This takes you straight down to **Faunarooska Castle** (**4h30min**). A ruined tower is all that is left of this fortified building.

Continue downhill to an iron gate, where you meet a narrow asphalt road. Turn right downhill, past the odd house, to a T-junction. Turn right here and skirt the hillside, passing some houses and joining the main road at the local SCHOOL. Continue for some 250m/yds, then turn left, back to the CAR PARK at **Fanore** (**5h30min**).

down to the right, into the lush valley, an extraordinary sight in this otherwise barren landscape. Keep straight on alongside a well-built stone wall when the trail peters out further down. Cross another stone wall at the end of this wall and carry straight on in the middle of the valley, heading through several walled fields and their iron gates. Finally you continue on a track, going through more gates and passing a house on the right.

Reach a junction near a FARM (**3h**), where you turn right onto the track up the hill. You have now joined a section of the **Burren Way**, as indicated by the waymarks. Flanked by old drystone walls, this green road ascends the hillside. From the CREST OF THE RIDGE (**3h15min**), a fine view of the green Caher Valley opens up below you. Note a ruined stone enclosure with two inner buildings *(Slí Bhoirne)* on your left, where the track begins to descend — the site of an ancient ring-fort.

Continue on the track down into the valley, where you join a narrow asphalt road and turn

Walk 15: CONNEMARA NATIONAL PARK

Distance: 2km/1.3mi; 1h
Grade: easy, with a climb of
80m/260ft. The walk is
suitable at any time of year.
Equipment: sturdy shoes
How to get there and return:
🚌 to/from the car park and
visitors' centre at the Connemara National Park near
Letterfrack (the 151km/94mi-
point on Car tour 9).

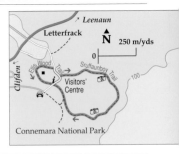

Extending around the boggy expanse of Glenmore
('large glen' in Gaelic), Connemara National Park
covers a number of mountains that form part of the
magnificent Twelve Pins range. These conical peaks
consist of quartzite underlain by less resistant schists
and grey and green marbles. There is an interesting
exhibition in the visitors' centre explaining the development of the Connemara landscape and wildlife. No time
checks are given for this circular walk — *do* take your
time to make the most of it. The route follows two
lovely nature trails that loop up at the visitors' centre,
taking in many diverse aspects of the park.

Start out at the **Connemara
National Park** VISITORS'
CENTRE: head northeast along
the signposted **Sruffaunboy
Nature Trail**, with **Diamond
Hill** (Bengooria) as a
mountainous backdrop. This
steep-sided mountain is one of
the quartzite cones typical of
the Twelve Pins area. Common
gorse, known locally as whins
or furze, covers the hillside
around you. It has a delicious
odour, rather like coconut, and
its yellow flowers bloom in
spring.
There is a large paddock on
your right where Connemara

*The Twelve Pins (Car tour 9), more traditionally known as the Twelve Bens.
This anglicised name is derived from the Gaelic* Na Benna Beola, *the peaks
of Beola, a mythological Celtic figure.*

ponies graze peacefully. This herd was introduced in the park in 1980 and is gradually increasing. Notice the old ridges running down through the pony paddock, testifying to past cultivation, when vegetables were still grown on the more fertile lowlands. Known as the 'lazy bed' system, furrows were dug in the waterlogged ground and ridges heaped up to improve drainage.

The gradient steepens as you climb along the trail. Cross a stile over a deer fence and follow the trail round a sharp hairpin bend to the right. There are sweeping vistas from this point over the coastal area to the west, extending around the deep inlet of Ballynakill Harbour. The lowlands are mostly covered in blanket bog, although traces of cultivation in the past are still evident. Cross a bridge over the **Sruffaunboy Stream**. The 'yellow stream' derives its name from the Gaelic *sruthán* (stream) and *buí* (yellow), referring to the colour of the water after floods. The following part of the walk leads through bogland where you are likely to see many of the acid-loving plants typical in this type of vegetation. Recross the deer fence and continue along the trail.

There are fine specimens of St Dabeoc's heath *(Daboecia cantabrica)* on the right-hand side of the trail as it swings to the right. Representing one of eight species of wild heather distributed in Ireland, it has large bell-shaped flowers. The trail leads back down to the Sruffaunboy and begins to follow its course downstream, the wet banks lined by shady willows. Keep right at a junction, to follow the trail past a pond, back to the VISITORS' CENTRE.

Go round the building, ignoring the start of the Sruffaunboy Nature Trail on your right and a turn on the left. Follow the road along the river, then turn left across a bridge. Take the right turn at the junction just beyond it. You have now reached the **Ellis Wood Nature Trail**. It winds its way through lush woodland with oak, ash, lime and other species, providing a shady canopy of leaves.

Soon you pass the old POWER HOUSE. Built in the 1920s, it used to generate hydroelectricity for the Letterfrack Industrial School. Continue along the trail as it winds up through dense woodland. From the southern section of the trail there are good views down the wooded hillside. Take the right turn at the AUDIO-VISUAL THEATRE, to head back towards the VISITORS' CENTRE and car park (about **1h**).

Walk 16: ALONG KILLARY HARBOUR TO ROSROE

See photographs page 48
Distance: 14.2km/8.9mi; 3h55min
Grade: moderate, with a climb of 190m/620ft. Suitable at any time of year.
Equipment: sturdy shoes, water, picnic
How to get there and return: 🚌 to/from Killary Harbour. From Kylemore Abbey, follow the N59 east towards Leenane (also spelled Leenaun). Pass a left turn signposted 'Tully Cross/Connemara Loop' *and* the next turn-off left, 250m further on. Continue for another 150m, to a small quarry on the right, where you can leave your car (the 164km/102mi-point on Car tour 9).

Carved out by glacial erosion over millennia, Killary Harbour (*An Caoláire Rua*) is regarded as the only real fjord in Ireland. Flanked by steep-sided mountains, this magnificent arm of the sea runs inland for about 16 kilometres/10 miles. This lovely walk takes you along the southern shore to an old deserted hamlet and then along a 'green road' to Rosroe, a tiny fishing village near the harbour mouth.

Start out at the small QUARRY ON THE N59: walk back along the road and take the right turn almost immediately. This narrow asphalt road takes you through bogland; on the right there are pleasant views over the wooded valley of the **Bunowen River**. A few houses line the sides of the road. **Killary Harbour** gradually comes into view, with the steep velvet-covered slopes of the **Mweelrea Mountains** as a backdrop. Note the mussel-beds in the water; fresh Killary mussels are a speciality of the region — not to be missed. Pass a right turn down to the PIER (**45min**).

Continue through an iron gate on the track ahead. Go through another iron gate; immediately beyond it there is a small water-fall on the left and a concrete bridge across the **Owenear-haghbeg** (**55min**). More mussel-beds come into view beyond another iron gate. You pass an ABANDONED COTTAGE on the left, framed by large rhododendrons (**1h10min**). The ruined houses that are scattered on the hillside to your left belong to the deserted hamlet of Foher *(Fothair)*; just one house is still intact.

Stay ahead on the 'green road' along the stone wall, leaving the hamlet up on the left; you will be visiting it on your way back. Go through some low stone walls and continue straight ahead on the old trail, now stone-laid in places. This green road affords splendid views out over Killary Harbour as it undulates gently along the slopes on your left. Swinging inland, your route begins to rise slightly, before passing a walled-in field on the right. You gradually descend to the

road at **Rosroe**, where you turn right and reach the quay near the MOUTH of **Killary Harbour** (**1h55min**). Turn back and walk along the road for about 15 minutes, until it bends right above **Little Killary Bay**. Leave it here and go left, through a wooden gate. Now climb the hillside alongside a power line, making for the obvious pass, with a scree-covered escarpment on your left. Reach the PASS (**2h35min**) and stop for a moment to catch your breath and enjoy the beautiful view from up here.

Now descend the gully beyond the pass, with a stone wall on your right. Leave the gully when the power line swings right and squeeze through the wire-mesh fence on your right. Follow the wall that skirts the hillside for a few paces, then turn left through a small rusty iron gate. Keep close to the stone wall at first, then descend the hillside diagonally, roughly following the power line, to reach **Foher** (**2h45min**). Take a break to explore what is left of this once thriving little community, superbly sited overlooking the harbour. In this peaceful setting it is hard to imagine the hardships the villagers faced in the past. Then go straight down the hillside, to rejoin your outward route. Turn right and retrace your steps back to the small QUARRY ON THE N59 (**3h55min**).

Walk 17: INISHBOFIN

See photograph page 48
Distance: 13.1km/8.2mi; 3h45min
Grade: moderate, with a climb of 250m/820ft overall. Suitable at any time of year, but avoid misty weather.
Equipment: sturdy shoes, water, picnic, bathing things (optional)
How to get there and return: 🚢 Dun Aengus mailboat from Cleggan to/from Inishbofin (details page 134). Cleggan can only be reached by 🚗 (the 138km/86mi-point

on Car tour 9).
Short walk: Western Inishbofin (7.2km/4.5mi; 2h; easy; ascent of 90m/295ft; equipment and access as above.) Follow the main walk for 1h28min, then turn right on the field track beyond the iron gate at North Beach. Follow it past a left turn, back to the scattered houses above Bofin Harbour. Turn right on meeting a T-junction and walk down the road. You meet your outward route again and turn left back to the pier.

According to legend, Inishbofin was discovered by two fishermen who lost their way in a violent storm and got stranded on its shores. As they ventured inland, they came upon a lake, where there was an old woman with a white cow. When the fishermen tried to catch the cow, they were both turned into white quartz rocks, and the woman disappeared in the lake. And so this peaceful haven (now with a mere 200 inhabitants) was called 'White Cow Island' — *Inis Bó Finne* in Gaelic.

Start out at the PIER on **Inishbofin**. Turn left on the narrow asphalt road and follow it along **Bofin Harbour**, past any right turns. When you reach the last house, keep straight ahead on the grassy track, ignoring another right turn. Shortly after going through an iron gate, the beautiful sandy beach of **Trá Gheal** comes into view down

on the left (**35min**). *(Unfortunately, there are treacherous undercurrents along this coast, especially at low tide, so swimming is **extremely dangerous**.)* Across the sea, the completely deserted neighbouring island of Inishshark rises out of the blue waters.
Continue along the grassy track until it swings to the right and becomes stony

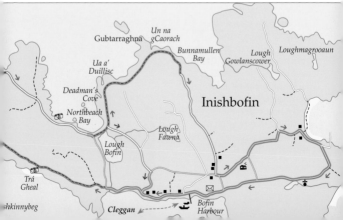

underfoot. Leave it here and head straight for the edge of the cliff, with the promontory of **Dún Mór** rising on your left in the west of the island. The sea has carved out a deep inlet bounded by sheer rock faces at the cliffs. Turn right and follow the cliff-top northwards. If you keep a bit inland, away from the edge, the going is much easier. The cliffs begin to diminish as you skirt **Royal Oak Cove**, where *The Royal Oak*, a large sailing ship, foundered at the beginning of the 18th century.

Continuing north, the rocky shore gently descends towards the **Stags of Bofin**, three islets off the west coast. Watch for a gravel track on your right as you reach the tidal rocks just opposite the islets (**1h**). Head for this track and turn right along it, through moorland. You pass two houses and go through an iron gate, before skirting **Northbeach Bay**. When you reach **North Beach**, a shingle ridge separating the bay from **Lake Bofin**, turn left across it (**1h25min**). Go through the iron gate at the end of the beach (**1h28min**) and turn left uphill, ignoring the track to the right. *(But the Short walk turns right on this track.)*

Climb the grassy hillside, cross over a saddle and descend to the coast near the cliffs at **Deadman's Cove**. Turn right along the rough shore, keeping slightly above it. You skirt another cove (**Ua a' Duillisc**) as you progress towards Gubatarraghna, a tongue of land punctuated with tidal rocks and some islets. Go round yet another cove (**Ua na gCaorach**) to reach **Bunnamullen Bay**. Skirt its

shore for about 10 minutes, then climb south into the hills. Cross a small bog where turf is cut and meet a TRACK (**2h15min**).

Follow this track through the hills, with Lough Fawna coming into view on the right. You pass some houses and go through an iron gate, before coming to a T-junction. Turn left on the small tarmac road and ignore a right turn almost immediately. Keep left at a fork not far beyond the island's power station. This tarmac lane takes you past a left turn by some houses and down to a beautiful sheltered BEACH (**3h05min**). On a fine summer's day this is perfect for swimming.

Leaving the beach behind, follow the road back into the hills. Pass an old ruined CHURCH down in the valley on your left, with a SMALL LAKE nearby (**3h20min**). The road takes you straight back to **Bofin Harbour**, where you pass the quay on the left before regaining the PIER (**3h45min**).

Walk 18: CROAGH PATRICK

Distance: 7km/4.4mi; 3h45min

Grade: strenuous, with a steep and slippery ascent of 750m/2460ft and an equally strenuous descent. *A word of caution:* keep strictly to the path and do not climb on wet or foggy days.

Equipment: walking boots, wind/waterproof jacket, walking stick, water, picnic

How to get there and return: 🚌 450 (Westport-Louisburgh-Killadoon service) to/from Murrisk (Croagh Patrick). Or 🚗: Murrisk is on the main coastal road R335, about halfway between Louisburgh and Westport. The large car park is on the south side of the road, opposite the turn-off to Murrisk Friary (the 41km/25mi-point on Car tour 10).

NB: Some 50,000 people climb Croagh Patrick every year, so weekends are generally best avoided. A national pilgrimage to Croagh Patrick takes place on the last Sunday in July (Reek Sunday), with thousands of people climbing the mountain to celebrate mass on the summit. There are public toilets at the car park, near the saddle and on the summit.

Croagh Patrick (*Cruach Phádraig*) is an isolated cone-shaped mountain rising up to 764 metres/ 2506 feet on the southern shore of Clew Bay. It is Ireland's holy mountain, where St Patrick spent forty days in the year 441 in prayer and fasting. From the summit there is a magnificent panoramic view over island-studded Clew Bay and the wild inland mountains.

Approaching the summit of Croagh Patrick.

breath, enjoying the magnificent view over Murrisk and Clew Bay.

The path swings to the right and continues round the back or southern side of **Lugnademon**. The view of Clew Bay is now concealed, but the Mweelrea Mountains, Sheeffry Hills and Partry Mountains can be seen rising inland. Awe-inspiring Croagh Patrick begins to tower ahead and, although you may wonder how on earth you are going to ascend its steep scree-covered slopes, the crowds will keep you going!

At the foot of the mountain you come to the First Station (**Leacht Benain; 2h10min**). When pilgrims reach this point, they walk round the cairn seven times, reciting seven Our Fathers, seven Hail Mary's and one Creed.

From here the toughest part of the climb begins — an extremely stiff uphill slog. Take your time, resting occasionally. Follow the outline of the path up through the scree. But leave the direct route up to the summit when the gradient increases appreciably, to avoid the steepest section of the hillside; veer to the right on a minor path. This path soon bends left and rejoins the direct route, ascending quite steeply to the SUMMIT of **Croagh Patrick** (**2h40min**). The breathtaking panorama from up here is more than ample reward for the strenuous ascent. The summit oratory is usually locked, but you can sit on its steps and shelter from the wind while you picnic. Descend the same way to the **Murrisk** CAR PARK (**3h45min**).

Start out at the upper end of **Murrisk** CAR PARK: follow the crowds uphill along the tarmac lane to an INFO BOARD, then climb some steps. When you reach the white STATUE OF ST PATRICK (**5min**), the serious climbing begins. Ascend the wide stony path, soon going through a wooden gate. On your right there is a good view of Lugnademon, a hilltop east of Croagh Patrick at a height of 510m/1673ft. The gradient eases as you reach a broad SADDLE between the summit on the left and Lugnademon on the right (**1h30min**). Take a break here to catch your

Walk 19: KINGS MOUNTAIN AND BENBULBIN

See also photograph page 55
Distance: 8.9km/5.5mi;
3h20min
Grade: Moderate-strenuous,
with a climb of 340m/1115ft.
Quite easy underfoot, but with
some wet and boggy sections.
Since most of the walk heads
cross country, a reasonable
sense of orientation is required.
Suitable all year round, but *not*
when there is low-lying cloud
or mist.
Equipment: walking boots,
wind/waterproof jacket,
walking stick, water, picnic;
compass an advantage
How to get there and return:
🚗 to/from Glendarragh, a
boggy basin east of Benbulbin.

From Sligo head north for
13km on the N15. Turn right
at Mullaghnaneane crossroads
(the 45km/28mi-point on Car
tour 11) on the lane signposted
to Ballintrillick. After 2.2km/
1.4mi turn right again at a
crossroads, now passing below
Benbulbin's northern escarpment. Cross Luke's Bridge
after another 2.2km/1.4mi,
ignoring a left turn almost
immediately. Climb the road
alongside the river for another
800m/0.5km, to reach a flat
concrete bridge where the
tarmac ends. Park near the
bridge, taking care not to block
the tracks used by the turf
cutters.

As you travel along the N15 between Sligo and Bun-
doran, a fluted, steep-sided limestone plateau rises
prominently in the landscape. Divided by deeply carved
glens, this giant flat-topped buttress has no distinct
summit. But some projecting spurs or promontories
appear as mountains in their own right, most notably
Tievebaun, Benwiskin and Benbulbin on the northern
escarpment. Immortalised in the poetry of Yeats,
Benbulbin (*Binn Ghulbain;* 'Peak of Gulba') forms the
western nose of the massif, while Kings Mountain rises
above the southern escarpment. The treeless limestone
massif is famous for its rare flora, including the fringed
sandwort *(Arenaria ciliata)* and alpine saxifrage
(Saxifraga nivalis).

Start out on the rough stony
track on the far side of the
CONCRETE BRIDGE at
Glendarragh: head south
alongside the stream, passing a
right turn almost immediately.
Note the traditional turf
cuttings on either side of the
track. You are aiming for the
stream that cascades down the
gully at the head of the valley,
descending from the lowest
point on the plateau. As the
track peters out, pick your way
south towards the bottom of

the hill, avoiding wet ground.
Rejoin the stream and follow it
steeply uphill. The vigorously
cascading stream suddenly
disappears, then later reappears
— a common phenomenon in
limestone terrain, where
underground streams permeate
the karst. Proceed up through
the gully to gain the PLATEAU
(**55min**).
Emerging from the gully, veer
slightly to the right (195°). As
you cross the limestone
plateau, covered in ling and

127

On the slopes of Benbulbin

Mountain (also known as **Finn McCool's Table**; 462m/ 1515ft; **1h25min**). There is a splendid view over the fertile coastal plain around Sligo, with Drumcliff Bay and Sligo Harbour in the southwest, backed by the flat-topped hill of Knocknarea topped by Queen Maeve's Cairn. East of Sligo lies beautiful Lough Gill, framed by wooded hillsides.

Descend from the summit the way you came, avoiding a gully to the northwest which is badly eroded. You are basically contouring round the rim of the plateau, heading northwest. Aim initially for the flat summit of Cartronwilliamoge, almost due north (350°); it's the highest point to the north; you can't miss it. As you approach **Cartronwilliamoge**, the trig point atop Benbulbin comes into view in the northwest. Don't climb Cartronwilliamoge; skirt its south side, leaving the summit on your right, to reach the broad RIDGE stretching to Benbulbin (**2h**). From here you enjoy a fantastic bird's-eye view to the northeast, over the boggy basin far below, with steep-sided Benwiskin rising on the far side. Head northwest along the crest of the ridge to the concrete trig point atop **Benbulbin**'s broad SUMMIT (526m/1725ft; **2h20min**). The views from here are not quite as good as from Kings Mountain.

Retrace your steps along the ridge back to the foot of Cartronwilliamoge and skirt it to the right, to pick up your outward route. Descend the gully that you climbed originally and return through the bog to the CONCRETE BRIDGE at **Glendarragh** (**3h20min**).

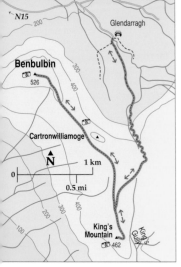

sphagnum moss, watch out for the many pits, probably remnants of the 19th-century barite mines. Off to the left you can see the TV mast atop the summit of Truskmore. Keep to the right of the upper reaches of **King's Gully** running due south and head straight across the undulating plateau towards Kings Mountain, which gradually comes into view ahead. Reach the base of the hill and climb the gentler eastern flank up to the SUMMIT of **King's**

Walk 20: SLIEVE LEAGUE

Distance: 12.1km/7.6mi; 5h15min

Grade: moderate-strenuous, with an ascent of 640m/2100ft overall. A fine clear day is best in order to follow the route easily; avoid wet or misty weather. Do *not* attempt if low cloud covers the summits.

Equipment: walking boots, wind/waterproof jacket, walking stick, water, picnic

How to get there and return: 🚗 via Teelin to/from the large car park at Amharc Mór (the 54km/33mi-point on Car tour 12).

Shorter walk: Circuit below Slieve League (10.3km/6.4mi; 4h40min. Moderate-strenuous, with an ascent of 590m/1935ft overall. Grade, equipment and access as above). Omit the

Mists hanging over the Cliffs of Bunglass

ascent to the summit; at the cairns (2h05min) turn right down the pilgrim's path, picking up the main walk again at the 2h40min-point.

S lieve League (*Sliabh Liag*; 'Mountain of the Flag-stones') looms dramatically over north Donegal Bay, with sheer rock faces plummeting down the rugged coast to the roaring sea. This ascent follows the classic route from Amharc Mór ('The Great View'), a superb vantage point overlooking the Cliffs of Bunglass, along the crest of the mountains and to the summit of Slieve League. Your return route is by an old Pilgrims' Path that gradually winds its way down to Teelin, from where you follow the road back up to Amharc Mór.

Start out from the end of the road at **Amharc Mór**: ascend the well-trodden path as it winds up to the first hill, **Scregeighter** (308m/1010ft; **30min**). Most tourists turn back here, but stay ahead on the rough path, to make your way along the cliff-edge to the next rise — **The Eagles Nest** (323m/1059ft; **45min**). The path splits occasionally and is rather steep and badly eroded in places, but it should pose no problems. On your left there are breathtaking views over the escarpment; on the right is

Teelin Bay. Looking back the way you came you can make out the signal tower on Carrigan Head.

Descend slightly from The Eagles Nest, then climb again, to contour the slopes of **Crockrawer** (435m/1427ft; **1h20min**) on its landward (eastern) side. The route continues along the crest of a ridge plummeting precipitously on both sides (keep to the landward side to avoid exposure). This hair-raising high-level stretch, with a yawning abyss on either side, really lives up to

129

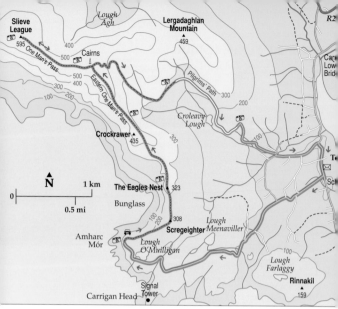

its name — much more so than the relatively broad One Man's Pass encountered later. (Perhaps the names were mixed up some time in the past, since this ridge is also called the 'Eastern One Man's Pass'.)

From the ridge you can clearly see your return route descending through the valley on the right. You reach a broad PLATEAU, where you come upon a number of CAIRNS (**2h05min**). This is where the Pilgrims' Path comes up the mountain from the right. (*The Shorter Walk turns right here.*) Continue past the cairns here, walking west across the narrowing ridge — **One Man's Pass**. From here you have fine views of Lough Agh down on the right, set in a corrie. From the trig point on the SUMMIT of **Slieve League** (595m/1952ft; **2h25min**) there are magnificent panoramas over much of Donegal and Donegal Bay. Return the way you came to the CAIRNS (**2h40min**) and swing slightly left, to descend into the bare saddle to the east.

Soon you pick up the **Pilgrims' Path**, which is rough and stony at the outset. As you descend there are fine views over the bays of Teelin and Donegal. The path gradually improves, crosses a stream, then swings left to the other side of the valley. Here a motorable track comes underfoot and you cross another STREAM (**3h10min**). Croleavy Lough is seen down in the flat valley on your right. Continue on tarmac as you go round a hairpin bend to the right. When you reach a T-junction, turn right across the BRIDGE (**3h40min**). Turn left downhill just beyond it and descend the road past a couple of right turns, to meet the main road in **Teelin** that you drove along earlier. Turn right here and walk past a rustic pub, to the junction by the SCHOOL (**4h**). Turn right again and ascend this road past the occasional house, ignoring any turnings. Go through the iron gate as you leave the last houses behind and continue along the road back to **Amharc Mór** (**5h15min**).

130

Walk 21: THE GIANT'S CAUSEWAY

Distance: 7.3km/4.5mi; 2h20min

Grade: easy, with a climb of 160m/525ft overall. On a wet day, the path can be muddy in places.

Equipment: sturdy shoes, wind/waterproof, water, picnic

How to get there: 🚌 172 (Ballycastle-Portrush bus) to the Giant's Causeway bus stop (main road). Or 🚗 to the car park and visitors' centre at the Giant's Causeway (the 101km/ 63mi-point on Car tour 13; www.giantscausewaycentre. com). There is an entrance fee.

To return: 🚌 172 from Dunseverick Castle; motorists alight from this bus at the Giant's Causeway main road bus stop, to pick up your car.

Short walk: Giant's Causeway circuit (2.9km/ 1.8mi; 55min. Easy. Equipment, access as above; return from the same place). Follow the main walk via The Organ to the Shepherd's Steps. Turn right at the top along the cliff-top path and follow it back to the visitors' centre. (Or shorten the walk even further, by taking the shuttle bus to the 15min-point.)

NB: The lower cliff path, which is still shown on some maps, is prone to landslides and *permanently closed* east of The Organ.

Associated with the legendary Finn MacCool, the Giant's Causeway is famous for its polygonal rock formations — nearly 40,000 columns of dark basalt jutting out into the sea. They were formed when volcanic lava erupted some 60 million years ago. As the lava cooled at a very steady rate, it solidified into crystalline columns— mostly hexagonal in shape. For more than 300 years, the Giant's Causeway has been a major tourist attraction, and a UNESCO World Heritage Site since 1986. But even in August you can quickly escape the hoards of tourists from all over the world by following this scenic cliff-top walk.

To begin the walk, go from the bus stop or car park through the *GIANT'S CAUSEWAY VISITORS' CENTRE* and exit by the back doors. (If the centre is closed, just walk round to the back of the building.) Walk down the asphalt road to the shore, ignoring the start of the cliff-top footpath up on your

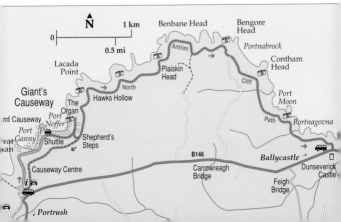

The Giant's Causeway

right. Pass **Great Stookan**, a promontory on your left, and follow the road round **Port Ganny**, with sheer cliffs rising on your right. The road ends at the **Giant's Causeway** (**15min**; there is a shuttle bus from the visitors' centre to this point). Explore the strange rock formations, with the **Grand Causeway** forming the biggest platform jutting out into the sea. Then continue from the turning circle through the **Giant's Gate**, a gap in the basalt columns. Follow the shoreline footpath round **Port Noffer**, past a large boulder known as the **Giant's Boot**. When you reach a junction, continue ahead for a moment, to see **The Organ** — vertical 'pipes' (basalt columns) on the cliff-face to your right (**25min**).

Now walk back to the junction and turn left up the **Shepherd's Steps**. Climb this flight of 162 steps, to emerge on the CLIFF-TOP PATH (**40min**). Turn left *(but turn right for the Short walk)* and follow it along the indented coastline, enjoying excellent views over the sequence of cliffs and bays. **Lacada Point** is the place where the Girona, 132

one of the galleons of the Spanish Armada, foundered in 1588. The ship remained undisturbed until it was discovered in 1968; its salvaged treasure is now exhibited in the Ulster Museum, Belfast.

Proceed round the edge of more promontories with sheer cliff-faces, all made up of 'sandwich cake' layers — symmetrical rows of basalt columns divided by bands of red laterite. You have to cross the odd stile as you follow the gently undulating path. Go round **Benbane Head** (**1h 30min**), the most northerly promontory on the Antrim coast. Once you're past **Bengore Head**, the wide bay of **Portnabrock** begins to unfold.

The path undulates to the next promonotory, **Contham Head**, beyond which **Port Moon** opens up, with its salmon fishery on the coast. Follow the coastal cliffs past **Portnagovna**, losing height gradually, until you meet the B146 opposite ruined **Dunseverick Castle**. The bus stops just where you leave the path (**2h20min**).

Walk 22: GLENARIFF FOREST PARK

Photograph page 64
Distance: 7.7km/4.8mi;
2h40min
Grade: easy, with a climb of
280m/920ft overall. Suitable
all year round.

Equipment: sturdy shoes,
wind/waterproof, water, picnic
How to get there and return:
🚌 to the car park at Glenariff
Forest Park (the 29km/18mi-
point on Car tour 13).

Luxuriantly green, with beautiful streams and gushing
waterfalls, Glenariff is one of the nine famous Glens
of Antrim. This scenic walk follows a waymarked trail
through forest and open mountainsides, with magnificent panoramas down over the glen to the coast.

Start out at the INFORMATION
BOARD at **Glenariff Forest
Park**: follow the red-marked
trail to the left. Keep left at a
junction almost at once, ignoring the red arrow/'Waterfalls
Walk' to the right and now
following BLACK WAYMARKS. At
the next junction, turn right —
down to a wooden footbridge
in the lush gorge, where a river
cascades boisterously over small
waterfalls, flowing through
DEEP POOLS rimmed with ferns
(**15min**). Return to the junction and now go straight
ahead. Cross the access road to
the forest park almost immediately and continue up the
waymarked trail through
luxuriant woodland, soon
enjoying fine views out over
the densely-wooded glen,
covered with maples, rowans
and alders. Turn right at a T-
junction, to reach a three-way
fork almost at once.
Turn left and follow the trail
towards the head of the glen.

Keep right at the next junction.
When you cross the rushing
Inver River and its tributaries
by some small bridges at the
head of the glen (**55min**), note
the lava rocks in the riverbed:
they were caused by the same
volcanic eruptions that built up
the Giant's Causeway.
The trail winds back up into
the forest before contouring
the hillside, affording panoramic views. Eventually the
trail begins to descend in steep
zigzags, then levels out and
runs ahead through a clearing.
Take a sharp right turn at a
junction and head straight
through the forest. Before
long, the track begins to zigzag
down into the densely-wooded
glen, eventually drawing near
to the Inver River that rushes
down the boulder-strewn
gorge beneath you on the left.
Turn left across a bridge and
left again at the JUNCTION just
beyond it (**1h50min**). Climb
the path along the steep side of
the valley, with the Inver down
on your left. Ignore a sharp
right turn and another (barred)
turn-off right, but turn right at
the next junction, passing a
large SHELTER on the left
(**2h30min**). Meet the bend of
a tarmac track and turn left
uphill. Continue past the
Glenariff Tea House, back to
the CAR PARK (**2h40min**).

133

Glenariff
Forest Park
Waterfoot
allymena
Glenariff
0
N
mi
1 km
Inver River

FERRY AND BUS TIMETABLES

FERRIES

Passage East Car Ferry
www.countywaterford.com/Waterford-travel_transport
Phone 00 353 (0)51 382480/382488
Continuous services; crossing time 10min
Mon-Sat 7.00-20.00, Sun 9.30-20.00,
summer (1.4.-31.9.) until 22.00

Bear Island Ferry
www.bereislandferries.com
Phone 00 353 (0) 27 75009
Regular services in season (21.6.-21.9.),
less frequent sailings 22.9-20.6; by
arrangement at other times.
From Castletown to Bear Island
Mon-Sat 9.00, 11.30, 13.30, 15.30, 17.30,
18.30, 20.30
Sun 12.30, 15.00, 17.00, 19.00, 20.00
From Bear Island to Castletown
Mon-Sat 8.30, 10.00, 12.30, 14.30, 16.30,
18.00, 20.00
Sun 12.00, 14.30, 16.30, 18.30, 19.30

Ferry from Portaferry across the 'Narrows' to Strangford
www.portaferry.info
Phone 00 44 (0)28 44 881637
Regular services (every 30min or so);
Mon-Fri first sailing 7.45, last 22.45;
Sat first sailing 8.15, last 23.15;
Sun first sailing 9.45, last 22.45;
crossing time 5min

'Galway Bay' Ferry to Inishbofin from Cleggan
www.inishbofinislanddiscovery.com
Phone Cleggan 00 353 (0)95 44878 or
Inishbofin 00 353 (0)95 45819
Departs Inishbofin *Tue, Fri, Sat* 8.15; *Mon,
Wed, Thu* 9.00; *Sun/bank hols* 10.00; *also
daily* 17.00 *(winter)*, 16.00 *(summer)*
Departs Cleggan *daily* 11.30; *Mon, Wed,
Thu, Sat, Sun* 18.45 *(summer)*, 16.45
(winter); Tue, Fri 19.30

BUSES

St Kevin's Bus
www.Glendaloughbus.com
Phone 00 353 (0)1 281 8119
Route: Dublin (Royal College of Surgeons
on St Stephen's Green) — Bray —
Glendalough; journey time 1h30min
Departs Dublin
Mon-Fri 11.30, 18.00
Sat/Sun/bank hols 18.00 (1.10-28.2), 19.00
(1.3-30.9)
Departs Glendalough
Mon-Fri 7.15, 9.45 (Jul/Aug only), 16.30
Sat, Sun/bank hols 9.45, 16.30 (1.10-28.2),
17.40 (1.3-30.9)

Killarney — Kenmare — Castletownbere (Castletown-Bearhaven)
www.buseireann.ie

Mon-Sat from 28.6-29.8 only
Departs Killarney (Service 270) 7.40, 15.00
Departs Kenmare (Service 282) 9.30, 16.10
Arrives Castletownbere 10.50, 17.30
Departs Castletownbere (Service 282)
11.00, 17.40
Departs Kenmare (Service 252) 12.45
Arrives Killarney 13.30

Bus 450 Westport — Murrisk (Croagh Patrick) — Louisburgh — Killadoon
www.buseireann.ie
Departs Westport
11.15 (a), 12.50 (b), 16.00, 16.00 (a), 18.05
Departs Murrisk (Croagh Patrick)
11.32 (a), 13.02 (b), 16.17, 16.17 (a), 18.22
Departs Louisburgh
11.50 (a), 13.25 (b), 16.35, 16.35 (a), 18.40
Arrives Killadoon
12.05 (a), —, —, 16.50 (a), —
Departs Killadoon
—, 12.10 (a), —, —, 16.55 (a)
Departs Louisburgh
8.00, 12.25 (a), 13.25 (b), 16.35 (c),
17.15 (a)
Departs Murrisk (Croagh Patrick)
8.18, 12.43 (a), 13.43 (b), 16.53 (c),
17.33 (a)
Arrives Westport
8.35, 13.00 (a), 14.00 (b), 17.10 (c),
17.50 (a)
(a) Thursdays only; (b) Tuesdays and Saturdays
only; (c) not Thursdays

Bus 172 Ballycastle — Portrush (via the Giant's Causeway)
www.nirailways.co.uk
journey time Ballycastle — Portrush 1h
*Departs Ballycastle (Marine Corner) towards
  Portrush*
Mon-Fri 7.30, 8.30, 8.45, 10.45, 12.45,
14.45, 15.45, 16.45, 17.45
Sat 10.45
Sun 9.30, 13.30, 15.45
Departs Dunseverick Castle
Mon-Fri 7.47, 8.55, 9.02, 11.02, 13.02,
15.02, 17.02, 18.02
Sat 11.02
Sun 9.55, 13.55, 16.10
Departs the Giant's Causeway (main road)
Mon-Fri 7.57, 9.05, 9.12, 11.12, 13.12,
15.12, 17.12, 18.12
Sat 11.12
Sun 10.05, 14.05, 16.20